TWAYNE'S WORLD AUTHORS SERIES

A Survey of the World's Literature

Sylvia E. Bowman, Indiana University

GENERAL EDITOR

CANADA

Joseph Jones, University of Texas

EDITOR

Bliss Carman

(*TWAS* 8)

TWAYNE'S WORLD AUTHORS SERIES (TWAS)

The purpose of TWAS is to survey the major writers —novelists, dramatists, historians, poets, philosophers, and critics—of the nations of the world. Among the national literatures covered are those of Australia, Canada, China, Eastern Europe, France, Germany, Greece, India, Italy, Japan, Latin America, New Zealand, Poland, Russia, Scandinavia, Spain, and the African nations, as well as Hebrew, Yiddish, and Latin Classical literatures. This survey is complemented by Twayne's United States Authors Series and English Authors Series

The intent of each volume in these series is to present a critical-analytical study of the works of the writer; to include biographical and historical material that may be necessary for understanding, appreciation, and critical appraisal of the writer; and to present all material in clear, concise English—but not to vitiate the scholarly content of the work by doing so.

Bliss Carman

By DONALD STEPHENS

University of British Columbia

Twayne Publishers, Inc.   ::   New York

For Desmond Pacey
who started it all
and
in memory of Bob
and of Dot

Preface

THIS BOOK is not an attempt to present a definitive discussion of the work of Bliss Carman, or to give a detailed examination of his life. A study that satisfied these two demands would be quite unnecessary because of the nature of Carman's work and the quality of his life. Eventually the reader discovers that Carman's poetry is marked by a peculiar kind of inconsistency, a lack of development, and a range of vague redundancy. The repetition in his work leads to repetition in a discussion of it. Carman's life was so much the product of tradition, and his attitudes so carved by the views of people he knew, that to focus attention on him is to study rather the quality of an age, and to consider the values and attitudes of other people.

For these reasons, the book has divisions that are a natural product of Carman's own work and life. The first chapter serves to give a general statement of his quality as a poet and as a man. The second chapter highlights those facts from which the various legends surrounding his life have come. It is important to differentiate the facts from the fiction; the conclusion drawn from studying a life so molded by attitudes of others, and so aware of the demands of a public image, is that Carman was more a man of "mask and myth" than an individual capable of original thinking and action. Carman was so much a part of the people he knew that to examine his life any more completely is to commit a disservice to him and to the intention of this book. There is really very little need for a more detailed study of his life; one can easily see why his literary executor, Lorne Pierce, did not complete the biography he planned to write about Carman. It would have made very dull reading. Nevertheless, because the quality of a life so much determines the kind of poetry a writer produces, the separate section on Carman's life is necessary here.

It is devoted to his life's more meaningful moments, in order to help the reader distinguish the masks Carman put on for himself, and the myths people created about him. It is hoped that a more accurate and clear picture of Carman as a human being is thus presented.

The third chapter, "Performance," is a discussion of his work. Here, because his reputation quite justly is maintained by his poetry, the focus is on the verse, with some reference to his prose. Again, because of the sameness of his work, a detailed study was not felt necessary. The chapter studies the chronological stages of his career with the reassertion of various forms and themes established early in his life. Specific poems in each volume of his verse show that Carman did not develop and change as a poet as he grew older; he was never able to draw together the strings of his imagination into an integrated statement. His poetry cannot to be divided into separate stages; instead, he vacillates in intention and idea.

The fourth chapter deals with the specific influences of other poets upon Carman's work. The most obvious mark of his poetry is its derivative quality; his most obvious technique was to use not only the ideas of other poets but also their method of expression. The influences themselves, and Carman's reading of these influences, must be recognized in order to bring about an understanding of his work.

The last chapter, "Conclusion," moves from an attempt at understanding Carman's work to an evaluation of it. There is, unfortunately, a double standard which circumscribes the discussion of most Canadian poets, and particularly, Bliss Carman. He played an important role in the development of Canadian poetry and is, along with Charles G. D. Roberts, nationally known as one of the leaders of the sixties group of poets. In recent years, some Canadian critics have given this position to Archibald Lampman and D. C. Scott, but Carman remains the poet of the group that most Canadians remember. He gave a great deal to Canadian poetry; he particularly stimulated interest in Canadian letters. Yet, by the standards of world literature, Carman's work is minor; his was a fine lyrical gift but it had been equalled and surpassed by others.

For the poems most commonly known, the Pierce edition of

Preface

Selected Poems has been used. Other quotations come from the original volumes, which more often provide the best text.

I would like to thank those who have so willingly given me their aid and advice in the writing of this book. My initial thanks go to Dr. Desmond Pacey of the University of New Brunswick who charted my original interest in Bliss Carman. My special thanks go to the students in my classes of Canadian Literature over the past five years, who have been a sounding-board for my ideas and who are partly responsible for the controlling attitude in this work. No doubt, my students in the years to come will make me re-evaluate the attitudes expressed here. But since I cannot wait for those years to pass, this study becomes a product of my interim thinking about Carman. Though I do not apologize for the attitudes expressed here, I do recognize the fact that they may change.

My thanks are due to the staff of the Bonar Law-Bennett Library at the University of New Brunswick, and to the library at Queen's University; to the Canada Council for a summer grant to complete the work; to John F. Hulcoop for recommendations during the making of the book; to Miss Joyce Zolles for typing the manuscript; and to my wife for her patience.

DONALD STEPHENS

University of British Columbia
Vancouver, British Columbia
August, 1964

Contents

Contents

Chronology

1861   Born on April 15 in Fredericton, New Brunswick.

1872   Begins six years at the Collegiate Grammar School in Fredericton under George R. Parkin.

1879   First poems are published in the *U.N.B. Monthly*, in Carman's first year at the University of New Brunswick.

1881   Carman graduates from the University of New Brunswick, with honors in Greek and Latin.

1882   Attends Oxford for a short while, and spends the rest of the school year in Edinburgh, Scotland.

1886   His mother dies; his father died the previous year.

1888   Finishes two years at Harvard, where he meets Richard Hovey, with whom he is later to collaborate in the *Vagabondia* series.

1893   *Low Tide on Grand Pré* is published.

1896   Meets Mary Perry King after he returns from a trip to England and France.

1904   Becomes poet-in-waiting to Mary Perry King, a relationship that is to continue until his death.

1920   Almost dies of illness in the Adirondacks.

1921   Goes on a cross-Canada tour, to thank his friends for their good wishes during his 1920 illness.

1929   Dies on June 8 in New Canaan, Conn.

1929   October 18, gravestone dedicated where the ashes are buried at the Forest Hill Cemetery in Fredericton.

1954   May, scarlet maple tree planted at Carman's grave, twenty-five years after his death.

1961   Centenary year of his birth passes almost unnoticed in Canada and elsewhere.

CHAPTER 1

Introduction

*Until you understand a writer's ignorance, presume yourself
ignorant of his understanding.*

IT is normally the proper discipline of critics that they should
subordinate their destructive impulses to a sublime acceptance
of Coleridge's view of the critical function. But in the case of Bliss
Carman, the character of the poet as well as the myth and the
legend that surround his name form obstacles to understanding
that no amount of humility can surmount. Bliss Carman seems
impossible; in fact, he seems impossible in three different ways. As
the poet, he is a sentimentalist, an eternal child. As the didactic
commentator upon the underlying significance of things, he is a
face in the crowd sucking all experience dry in the maw of his
philosophy. As a poet he is schizophrenic; his technique ranges
from the clumsiness of a grade school sentimentalist to passages of
eloquent description and rare sensitivity. But the impossibility
that characterizes him is that there appears to be no obvious ex-
perimental relation among his many aspects. In short, not only is
one tempted to admit that Carman is a "very minor poet," but also
to see in his poetry one of those cathartic moments when it is
possible to cease throwing sops to academic rectitude and to offer
instead a bloody sacrifice on the somewhat amorphous altar of
aesthetics.

But to damn Carman's poetry, no matter how decorously, because of the poet himself, is to miss entirely the nature of Carman's poetic contribution to Canadian letters. To identify the
poetry he wrote as Carman's philosophy, as his mouthpiece for all
mankind to hear, is a gross error, despite what appears to be an
apparent similarity of purpose. The poetry he wrote is not a
poetry of his time, depending on poet-in-action; it is, rather,
poetry depending on spirit-in-action. The conflicts he presents, the
world he sees, the pictures he paints, all are the essential representation of the conflict of the human spirit. Carman's poetry is not

the poetry of an age, or of a separate man, but is poetry produced by the spirit of many men. Carman was not an innovator; he was an imitator and a borrower. His poetry is essentially a verbal pattern in which the different qualities are strands borrowed from what was influencing him most at the time. For the most part these influences are from other poets, or from what Carman saw in the works of others; he was not always sensitive to the core meanings of the writers he admired and imitated. At other times he borrowed from his own experience, be it his dead mother, a lost friend, a nostalgia for home when he was alone in Edinburgh, a reading of Swinburne on a hill overlooking the St. John River, or twenty years under the influence of the Madame Blavatsky of his life, Mary Perry King. The reader's experience arising from all this change, all this variety, has the impact of a fascinating pattern; it remains true, therefore, that the poet belongs to the organization and presentation of experience rather than to its substance. When we examine the practical product of almost fifty years of poetry, we come face to face with the fractured configuration of Carman. If we are to understand the shape of the poetry we must first delineate the disparities in Carman as a character, as part of the legend and the man, and their effect on the experience that his poetry produces for readers today.

It appears firstly that Carman is a writer of violently fluctuating ability. Some of the poems simply ache with a kind of purple loquacity; clichés that could only be deliberate and images that could only be apologetic are legion. We need only see two examples to show how bad he can be:

> When night goes over the hill
> And dawn comes down the dale
> ("A Northern Vigil")

> Make me over, mother April
> When the sap begins to stir!
> ("Spring Song")

When there is emotion it is couched in terms of highly exaggerated tension, and the surface structure of individual poems is rarely artful. Yet there are moments when greater heights are reached that have rarely been attained in Canadian poetry. "Low

Tide on Grand Pré" is the best example of this; there are others, and individual lines suffice:

> And there is nothing more in this great world
> Than thou and I, and the blue dome of dusk
>
> I loved thee, Atthis, in the long ago,
> When the great oleanders were in flower
>
> How soon will all my lovely days be over
> And I no more be found beneath the sun,—

This is the poetry of a man who, when he wanted to, was able to capture in word, rhythm, and imagery, a nicely unified expression. Unfortunately, he did not always take such care.

It is easy to put Carman in with a group of poets, Canadian and otherwise, to discuss his affinities with the nineteenth century, and to leave him there. It is harder, but so much more interesting, to find what is behind his mask. Why did he borrow so much? In fact, why did he so consciously and obviously borrow? In one of his aspects Carman is most certainly a kind of Chaucerian innocent, but even this disguise is curiously incomplete. A satisfying integration of Carman's nature must therefore include more than his innocence, without denying that innocence as an element. The place to look for that integration is in the world he inadvertently created, the world of image in which he appears as one of the spiritual images. The bare bones of his world are made up of nature; he is part of that scene:

> Between the roadside and the wood,
> Between the dawning and the dew,
> A tiny flower before the sun,
> Ephemeral in time, I grew.
>   ("Windflower")

He is part of the landscape he sees; he is not, like many of the writers risen to fame in the latter years of Carman's life, staring at a landscape which stares back.

There is a curious tendency to downgrade the poetry of Bliss Carman because he always wrote in a fairly conventional manner. There is, often, even a slight tone of rebuke, as if he had been caught leading his public astray somehow, as though he should have done so much better. It is difficult to agree with this point of view, even though a reader may have different reasons to launch a tirade against him. He was born in Fredericton, New Brunswick, in 1861, when it was—and in many senses still is—a town of tradition; it would be strange indeed, if, from such a beginning, he had plunged immediately into abstract poetry or any other advanced type of poetry so common in the twentieth century. He could not then or ever produce anything else but what he did write.

It is a miracle that anyone growing up in an out-of-the-way place and in humdrum surroundings should ever decide to become a professional poet. The countryside needed a spokesman, but the emotions of the landscape had been expressed fifty years earlier by the English Romantic poets. The whole range of Carman's poetry—the chronological range—shows that his poetic structure is almost entirely built on organic images—flowers, vines, the seasons, such landscape features as grasses and water flow. It was his world, and it remained his world. He was constantly changing his ideas, his values, his ideals; he was always under the influence of some other human being, from the renowned dead to the very ordinary living. It would be pointless to itemize all the twistings and turnings he went through, or to analyze them; it would be especially difficult because a good many of them, on the evidence of publication dates, occurred simultaneously, or nearly so. One gets the feeling that like Yeats, but not quite with Yeats' enormous authority, Carman was willing to try anyone's bent and either to put his findings to use or to reject them. Among his influences one sees all the Romantics, but then, what artist of Carman's generation was not influenced by the Romantics? Emerson emerges, disappears, reappears, and then vanishes.

In the end, though, as must always be the case if basic talent is involved, the experiments, the influences, the working-around, began to channel themselves toward a consistent, comprehensive purpose. He would be the Canadian poet's poet! This was to be his special trademark. Infrequently, the later poetry is muralistic in derivation, but the poems belong more to the strong processional quality of the Romantics. But he died in 1929, and it was over. Perhaps it was over thirty, if not thirty-five, years before.

Introduction

Here is a poet who is revered in his own native city of Fredericton; yet no one knows the sculptor who did the bust in the university library foyer. Here is a man who never married, yet spent
almost thirty years of his life *en ménage* with Dr. and Mrs. Morris
King. Here is a man who was the unofficial poet laureate, yet
whom many Canadians never knew. What was he like? What was
the real man? At what point can we penetrate the masks Carman
assumed and the myths others created, in order to understand the
man who wrote the best stanza of nineteenth-century Canadian
poetry?

> Was it a year or lives ago
> We took the grasses in our hands,
> And caught the summer flying low
> Over the waving meadow lands,
> And held it there between our hands?

CHAPTER 2

Mask and Myth

IN order to grasp the differences between the mask and the man, the myth and the man, it is best to look first at Carman as fact has recorded him. He was born on April 15, 1861, and died on June 8, 1929; this life bridges the era between the last of the great Victorians and the new writers who evolved the complexities of twentieth-century poetry. During his lifetime no major poets appeared on the literary scene. Yeats had not yet attained his greatness; the grouping of poets—the Rhymer's Club, the Georgians, the War Poets—did little except show certain inadequacies in contemporary English verse; Eliot was still extremely *avant-garde* even toward the end of Carman's life. Poetry was in a state of fluctuation; there was no definite contemporary verse. Poets of the time, and Carman especially, could only look back to the past. His poetry is really a restatement of certain nineteenth-century poetic values. It could hardly be otherwise.

It was always, and ever would be, a world of county, queen, and empire in the Fredericton where Carman was born. The family loved tradition; in fact, they were concerned with retaining a link between their lives and the English past. Fredericton is in the county of *York* in *New Brunswick;* its main street is *Queen* Street; other streets are *Kings, Westmoreland, Regent,* and other names associated with monarchy. All the middle-class virtues were praised by the family: breeding, social position, material links with the past. Into this city and this family Carman was born.

He descended from John and Florence Carman who had settled, in 1631, on Long Island, New York, after arriving from England. They chose that part of America which reminded them most of home, and where the majority of their neighbors would be of good English stock. For one hundred and fifty years the family flourished in New York, but when the American Revolution took place—they would not call it the War of Independence—their love for England was their first duty and they moved to the nearest English stronghold, New Brunswick, in 1783. They first settled in Saint John where Richard Carman, the leading member of the family at the time, became one of the first grantees of the city. This strong Loyalist background was to continue to influence the Carmans for another hundred years, if not longer. In Saint John William Carman, the father of Bliss Carman, was born in 1804. If the Maritimes ever had a melting-pot city, Saint John was that city; in the first half of the nineteenth-century it was the place where the United Empire Loyalists came, where the European settlers came, where many races and philosophies mingled. Yet, curiously, there was little assimilation; the Loyalists remained alone because they wanted to; they had learned through bitter experience that in order to retain their belief and respect for things English they must separate themselves from other groups.

This Loyalist strain was not only on Carman's father's side. His mother's family were descended from the Reverend Daniel Bliss of Concord, Massachusetts, the great-grandfather of Ralph Waldo Emerson. The family was always associated with the law, both in New England and New Brunswick, and were renowned for their Loyalist leanings. Sophia Mary Bliss, daughter of George Bliss, was William Carman's second wife; her husband was many years her senior. Her sister was the mother of Charles G. D. Roberts.

So it was not into a pioneer family or into a family consciously seeking a new life, that Bliss Carman was born. This was a family where everything had its place, where time and tradition had molded a way of life, an attitude. And this attitude was not peculiarly Canadian; in fact, the only significant Canadian attribute of Bliss Carman is the place of his birth. His world was not one in which experiment was trusted; it was a world where the old was respected because it was old, where the new was challenged because it was new; it was beautifully and wretchedly middle-class. This was a world which had never recognized any breach with England. The poetry of Carman consequently never twisted itself out of the shape that made it; it belonged to the thousand-year tradition of England. His role as a poet was to bring continuity to

Canadian poetry, a continuity developed from the English tradition.

To talk of family and its influence, to mention ancestors and beliefs, is to move in rather shallow water; there are so many reactions to the past from the young and the new. But Carman was not one to reject the past, and rarely did he question its meaning; his questions were for his own time and involved the many changes going on around him.

It is in the home, the family, and the city of his youth that is found the strongest evidence of the respect for the past and for the English, Conservative, Anglican background. The house in which the Carmans lived in Fredericton was bare and almost antiseptic in appearance. There is still a Victorian dankness about it which is reflected by its dark color on the outside and its feeling of closeness on the inside. The outside was painted black—it is brown now—so that it could be easily and inexpensively cared for. The house is near to the street; the garden was, and is, closely confined. Inside, except for the light and well-proportioned living room, the house is a series of small rooms, crowded passages, dark woodwork. It is not like the early home of Charles G. D. Roberts which is large and spacious, open to air and light. The myth surrounding Carman includes the picture of a typical New England house—white painted clapboards, green shuttered windows—situated on the top of a hill overlooking a river; cornflowers are imagined growing at the edge of a rather formal garden filled with apple trees and birches, under which the poet sat and wrote his poems. Admittedly the river can be seen; it is nearby, but on the same level as the house. Carman talks of seeing the apple blossoms from his window, and the cathedral spire in the distance, but it is a separated picture, not part of his own immediate landscape.

The myth becomes real, however, in the city of Fredericton itself, a place where all the adjectives of romanticism can apply. Nestled on a flat plain on the side of the St. John River, the city is replete with stately houses and sections of the English town-house where the homes are built close to the street, side by side. The elms are statuesque and shading; the church spires pierce the sky. Softly rolling hills rise around the city; in the summer they become "blue remembered." There is little major industry; the air is sweet and clear. The river flows gently by; the wind is soft. It was a typically provincial city; there could be punts on the river, young men in white blazers, young girls in Renoir-blue picking flowers in quiet gardens where bees hummed.

Into this world Carman came, into a world where custom and habit had been established too long to ever change. It was a background which he could never escape—not that he ever wanted to—nor is it to be suggested that he should have. But his world was created before he came into it, and he easily and readily accepted it; he never questioned its values; he never argued with its concepts. For him it was an ideal world, rarely disturbed. Even though he may have become melancholy about his state, it was not because he was agitated by the condition of his world, for the most part; his melancholy was more another facet of his traditional world. His dissatisfaction was only directed at those people and those ideas which threatened to transfigure, or even change in a minor way, the world as he saw it and as he thought it to exist.

From childhood he accepted everything around him; he learned to acquire respect for the past, and for the values of his family. When he was older he continued to rely on others; Bliss Carman could not survive alone. His family and friends taught him respect for the past and for tradition; they taught him that breeding and family were important; they taught him to observe the rules of virtue, valor, integrity, and honesty. At times, too, they taught him to smile, sometimes even to laugh. And in their way they taught him how to survive; and it was a survival that depended upon others. Out of this background grew a boy, a man, and a poet, who could not subsist alone. There was one short time in his life when he did try to emerge; but his cultivated melancholy caught him and he returned. There is only one short time when his readers see him as he really was; the rest of the time he was so much supported by the people he knew; he so much needed the ideas and values of others that he could not separate himself. It was not his fault; it was the world in which he lived.

Typically, he was educated at first by a private tutor, and eventually entered the celebrated Collegiate Grammar School in Fredericton (1872–78) whose headmaster was George R. Parkin, later chairman of the Rhodes Scholarship Trust. This was a school which specialized in small classes, where the teaching was in the form of seminars and discussions, where there was a strong relationship between tutor and student. Parkin loved to teach and was an inspiring teacher. In a letter to H. D. C. Lee, Carman described Parkin as "one of the greatest teachers I have ever known, who gave me all my enthusiasm for learning and for poetry." [1] Carman came to the school with a traditional background of *The Book of Common Prayer*, Shakespeare, Milton, and Tennyson. To this Parkin added another tradition—the Greek and Roman classics—which became very important to Carman; he was to continue using them both for a frame and for allusion in all his poetry. At times, fortunately, Parkin moved outside the past and into the vigorous present; this was the age of Swinburne, Arnold, and Browning. Parkin would take a small group of boys for a walk up into the hills overlooking Fredericton and the river, and there he would read their contemporary poets to them. Carman felt that these hikes had given him some of the greatest pleasure in his life. Parkin had introduced him to the joy of reading, and he says: "And I for one have to thank you for a pleasure in life, almost the only one, that does not fail." [2] He dedicated his book, *The Kinship of Nature* to Parkin; it is from the writer, "For the service you did him is, next to the gift of life, the greatest that one man can render another." Carman, at first, resisted praise for those writing in his lifetime; but eventually, as he developed his own career as a poet, he learned to understand and appreciate them. Browning, particularly, was always a favorite of his. He said, toward the end of his life, that his favorite poet was Browning and that he was always indebted to Parkin for introducing Browning to him. No one knew better than Carman himself how easily he accepted the values of others, how easily he became a disciple. The years at the Collegiate School were happy ones; from there he moved on to the University of New Brunswick.

At the university, Carman continued to excel in studying the classics, and it was from them that he received the inspiration to write poetry. His first published verses, which appeared in the *U.N.B. Monthly*, were translations of Homeric hymns, and a few lines from Virgil and Horace. There is nothing that distinguishes these verses; rather, they are like so many produced by adolescent boys initially charmed by the ancient languages of the original. This interest in the classics was to stay with him all his life, to emerge finally into an interest in mythology, indicated in poems concerned with another time; *Sappho* and the *Pipes of Pan* are the most obvious examples. Here the imitation and borrowing is acceptable, for he was young; it is acceptable for a poet who is beginning to use models. The changes in word and diction show some promise; the choice of form shows a mind not ready to branch out on its own.

After graduating from the university in 1881, with honors in Latin and Greek, Carman spent a year at home in private reading. He did very little that year, but went on an occasional hike on the hills surrounding Fredericton. It was expected that a young man of his time would spend a year reading and catching up on things that he had been unable to do at the university. His reading had been rated "very poor" at the Collegiate School, and his performance continued to distress him at the university. The year spent at home was to make up for this lapse. The following year he went to Oxford, urged there by Parkin. He left Oxford quickly, for he was lonely and homesick, and ended up in Edinburgh, joining his friend, Herbert Pickard, Gilchrist Scholar from New Brunswick. Pickard urged him to take studies in mathematics, physics, and philosophy. The first two were completely alien to him; the philosophy he enjoyed.

But he did not like Edinburgh any better than Oxford; it was a dour and gray city, and he missed the warmth of the sun in New Brunswick and the profusion of color in nature there. In his letters at that time he shows an almost neurotic aversion for Edinburgh and looks back to New Brunswick with nostalgia. In letters to his mother, he recalls reading Browning in those hills over Fredericton; he almost wallows in a newly developed self-pity which was to stay with him, at varying intensities, throughout his life. He returned to Fredericton in late 1883. His visit to England and Scotland was a complete waste of time for him. He was too immature at that time to get pleasure from a different scene; the only impression the trip made on him was negative. He only stuck more closely to the roots of his past. He had not gone on the trip because he was looking for something new in experience. He had gone because it was expected of him—he had been urged to go.

He was glad to be home, but could not decide what to do with himself. For a while he taught in Parkin's school, but found it hard to communicate his love of classics to the students; he also worked for a while in a Fredericton law office, reading law. He then went to Maine where he worked with a surveying party. He could not settle down to one thing; all the early molding could not make him move in one direction; he had to go many ways before he decided what to do, and eventually, someone else had to do the deciding for him. It was his mother who encouraged him, and so he tried teaching, law, and engineering on her advice.

The influence of his immediate family was to end quickly, however. His father died in 1885, his mother in 1886, and he was free to do what he wanted. But he did not know what that was; the only thing he did know was that he wanted to go back to the university, to study more, to have the time to make decisions about his future and still use the time to advantage. He took advantage, too, of the role of the student: it was an easy way to avoid a decision about his life. He could study until someone came along to make a decision for him. He applied for a fellowship at Johns Hopkins where he was refused, but in the fall of 1886 he entered Harvard; his world was now beginning to open.

From 1886 to 1888 he studied English literature under Francis Child at Harvard, with the intention that he would eventually teach in a small college similar to the University of New Brunswick. He changed his mind, however, when he went to listen to Josiah Royce's lectures in philosophy; this changed his direction for a while. He was also writing some poetry of his own, and so he continued to vacillate, this time from poetry of his own to the study of English literature, to philosophy. He was acted upon, rather than acting. His past had not prepared him to take his own initiative; he was too easily influenced by the people he listened to, by the people he met. He would change course as a ship with sails changes tack according to the wind. He always needed an external influence upon him.

While at Harvard he met the American poet Richard Hovey, with whom he was to collaborate later in the *Songs of Vagabondia* series. Through Hovey, who gave him direction and encouragement to be a poet, he met other poets and people interested in writing: William Morten Fullerton, Tom Meteyard, Ralph Cram, Bertram Goodhue and others. His particular friend was Hovey and they reacted violently upon each other, to the advantage of both. They both had high opinions of each other's verses, and

Hovey urged Carman to start submitting his poetry to *The Harvard Monthly,* which began to publish the poems of both men. They were earnest and young, both around twenty-five, and considered themselves quite unique; after all, poets were rare in America at that time. Together they turned away from things academic—Hovey from studying Hebrew with an intention of entering the ministry, Carman from the pursuit of English literature and philosophy—and became practicing poets instead. It would be hard for one poet to survive alone; for two it would be easier. They complemented each other both in looks and attitude. Hovey was dark and muscular, Carman was fair and lanky. Again, the influence was on the latter; he was not doing the influencing. The aesthetic Carman, the pale youth, became a counterpart for Richard Hovey; for one who hated to go for walks of any duration, for one who enjoyed looking at a landscape but not trudging through it, it seems a paradox to have become a disciple of the "joys of the open road" and the co-author of the *Vagabondia* books. It was not his nature; but again it was his nature to follow a path that someone else had put ahead of him. Bliss Carman once told a crowd in the high school in Moose Jaw, Saskatchewan, that to hike and tramp in the woods was alien to his nature; he liked to observe nature, to sit and watch the tide, to take a full look at the landscape, but not to camp and hike. And yet, because of the *Vagabondia* series, there is the legend about his love for the open road; in "The Joys of the Open Road" these are enumerated. But even in this poem, lines such as

> A lover of books, but a reader of man,
> No cynic and no charlatan,
>
> Who never defers, and never demands,
> But smiling, takes the world in his hands,—

belie this picture of a man of the road, and a wanderer. Admittedly, he loved life in the country, but only from the open veranda, or from a rock overlooking the sea.

Richard Hovey took him to his parents' home in Washington, and during his vacations there, and with Charles G. D. Roberts in Nova Scotia, he started his career as a poet. From Royce at Har-

vard he had accepted a neat set of values by which he could justify his semi-mystical contemplation of nature, and his concept
that the good and the beautiful somehow survive and work themselves out in the universe. From Francis Child, the authority on
the ballad, came the interest in the rollicking form which was to
become the basis for the *Vagabondia* series.

Carman came closest to his real self on his trips around Nova
Scotia. In the bosom of his family, and with his cousin, Charles G.
D. Roberts, he spent part of the summers there. Windsor, Nova
Scotia, was the home of Roberts, who was then a professor of
English at King's; it was only a few miles from the country made
famous by Longfellow's *Evangeline*. Carman loved that part of
the world, and enjoyed wandering around, sitting by the rivers
and the sea. It was here that he finished the greater part of his
volume of poetry, *Low Tide on Grand Pré*, published in 1893; the
title poem of this volume, however, had been completed while he
was at Harvard, and was first published in *The Atlantic Monthly* in
1887. This volume, peculiarly, shows Carman at his most original.
As he went farther away from home and family he reached out his
hand to others; there was always someone to take him in, someone
who liked to lead as much as Carman liked to follow. But in the
land he knew best, Carman was his most sincere, simple, and least
artificial.

Carman decided after leaving Harvard that he would do magazine work, which would enable him to keep in contact with what
was being done around him by his contemporaries and which
would give him impetus and encouragement to write his own
poetry. He knew he needed urging, and to dwell in a world where
things were being written and published was a natural setting for
his nature. He first worked on the New York *Independent* where
he had some decisions to make about the poems to be published;
while there he published poems of Pauline Johnson, Archibald
Lampman, Duncan Campbell Scott, and other Canadians. He
also worked for a while on the *Literary World, Current Literature, The Outlook* and *The Cosmopolitan,* and later held his most
distinguished position on *The Atlantic Monthly* where he did edi-
torial work (of no distinction, incidentally). However, the position he enjoyed most was on *The Chap-Book* in Boston, where he

worked from 1894 to 1897 when the magazine moved from Cambridge to Chicago. These years he loved. He was with people he
enjoyed and with friends he had known for some time. The first of
the *Vagabondia* books established him as a successful and notable
poet; the year before, the publication of *Low Tide on Grand Pré*
had attracted interest. With people like Cram and Goodhue,
Lloyd Osborne, Sara Wiley and Louise Imogene Guiney around
him, he and Hovey had started a new era in North American
letters. And it was at this time, after returning with Goodhue from
a walking tour in England and France in 1896, that he met Mrs.
Mary Perry King.

Aside from his mother, the greatest and most sustained female
influence on Carman's life was that of Mary Perry King. It was a
mixed influence exerted by a domineering and cultivated woman.
He spent much time in the company of Mrs. King and her husband, Dr. Morris King, during the ten years after meeting them.
In 1907–08 he went to Boston where, with Mrs. King, he wrote
The Making of the Personality. He spent the rest of his life either
living with the Kings or living close to them. In 1908 he went to
live in New Canaan, Connecticut, a small town close to Long Island Sound. In the summer he went to the Catskills—always close
to the Kings or in their company. Mrs. King was the closest person
to Carman in the last thirty years of his life; at his death she portrayed the role of his widow. The relationship between them is
shadowed by the resentments of many of Carman's friends who
objected to Mrs. King's complete control of him. What then, are
the facts of this relationship; where is the myth? where is the
truth?

These questions are difficult to answer, but they can be partly
answered in truth so that the rest does fall into place. Mrs. King
liked the role she could play with Carman; she pictured herself as
his patron in the eighteenth-century tradition. She gave him
money, she gave him food and lodging; she inspired him to write
—admittedly it is dreadful prose and almost equally bad poetry.
Carman was infatuated with her, of that there can be no doubt;
he genuinely adored her. And it was, in a sense, a practical relationship. She needed someone to command, someone to look up to
her; Carman needed someone to advise him, someone to mother

him, someone to look after him; he also needed someone to love. But it was not so much physical satisfaction that Carman was looking for; he wanted and needed a love that had a strong spiritual quality. He found all this in two women in his life: the first was his mother; the second was Mary Perry King.

There are various interpretations of the relationship between the two. A few of Carman's friends saw it as merely a kind of mother-child relationship: she was a woman who liked to help artists; the family had money, and she had little else to do. Others saw Carman as unhappy in New Canaan in proximity with the Kings; they feel that his nature was to give in to Mrs. King's whims because she had helped him out so much financially.[3] Still others see them as lovers, with Carman slowly growing away from the woman who supported him in many ways. Others have seen Carman as a man who took the best of his world because he enjoyed the comforts which Mrs. King offered to him. The facts support some of these theories; together they paint a rather full picture.

The attraction between the two people initially started because they had something in common, and because it was Carman's nature to easily accept the attitudes of others. Mrs. King was a strong woman; she enjoyed a following. They had a mutual respect for the work of Henrietta Hovey, Richard Hovey's wife. Mrs. Hovey was a student of Delsarte, and had influenced Carman greatly; he merged her philosophy of the personality with his concept of the trinity of personal behavior from the Greeks, in Truth, Beauty, and Goodness. Carman had, by the time he met Mrs. King, established some reputation through his books, brochures and broadsheets. He was impressed with her teacher, Mrs. Hovey, with her ideas of Unitrinianism. He could give to her school some of the tone that she felt it needed; his handsome and aesthetic appearance easily charmed many of the young women who went to Mrs. King's school of Personal Harmonizing. Mrs. King needed a man like Carman to impress these beautiful and talented—and wealthy—girls who came for her courses in personal development. Together, Carman and Mrs. King wrote *The Making of the Personality*, and after its publication in 1908 he was never far from her side as an active associate in her ideas. Carman lived near the King estate, "Sunshine House" in New Canaan, and in the summer lived at "Ghost House," one house away from the King home, "Moonshine."

It was, first of all, Mrs. King's philosophy which Carman admired. He wrote to many of his friends through the years that Mrs. King's whole concept of life had captured him. "I see here a great and new philosophy and scientific truth of value beyond telling, to education of coming men and women; and I cannot lose one chance of helping it forward," [4] he said. The philosophy was a simple one, and one that Carman with all his traditional upbringing could easily appreciate and understand.

The philosophy of Unitrinianism, an old concept derived from the Greeks, offers serenity to the individual through a belief in the symmetry of all things. A person's life should be an equal balance of the physical, emotional, and mental aspects of his personality. To gain this balance is a chief goal. Mrs. King held seminars in her home to educate people concerning the harmonizing of the personality, and the liberating of the emotional nature of man through expression in poetry, music and dancing. In this philosophy there is no division between the spirit and the body, as there is in orthodox Christian philosophy, but a full integration of the mind, spirit, and the body. To strengthen the body alone, without also working on the spirit and the mind, is a deception; the three must develop together. In his poetry, Carman extended this into a belief in the essential unity of Nature, Man, and God and wrote *The Kinship of Nature* as his prose statement of this idea. Personal happiness comes to those who look at life in this way. Those who seek unity in things achieve a full and richer life. There are moments when a man's intuition tells him that these things are achieved; there are moments when he glimpses beyond his world.

There is, no doubt, something strange about this philosophy; it appears watery, with little intrinsic basis for belief. Rather, its basis seems to lie in a strange intangible, not even strong enough for an absolute faith. The personal relationship between Mrs. King and Carman shows that both were able to put a great deal of meaning into ordinary things, that they enjoyed dramatizing an idea or a situation. Initially, they met on common ground because of their respect for Mrs. Hovey's ideas, but Mrs. King captivated Carman with other concepts that would bind them together into a stronger and more meaningful relationship. They were born a day apart, and to Mrs. King this was an important manifestation of their need to be together; in a sense, it controlled the relationship that was to last for almost thirty years.

It is difficult at any time to describe, let alone explain, the relationship between a man and a woman. Each one has its own peculiar quality. Though the twentieth century is an age in which the platonic relationship between a man and a woman is disparaged and disbelieved, when innuendoes are made about the man's masculinity and the woman's femininity, the variety of human experience surely shows that any kind of a relationship can exist. There is no proof to reinforce the idea that Mrs. King and Carman were lovers. Aside from his feminine mannerisms, there is nothing to prove that Carman was a homosexual. Evidence available proves only that the two people were very close; mundane as it may be, they were merely "kindred spirits." Carman's letters and poems show that he would not cultivate a relationship that would be morally wrong, and his traditional background showed him that adultery would be a great and cardinal sin.

Mrs. King, however, was a most peculiar woman, and became very possessive about Carman, insulted his friends, and despised any call to take him away from her. When he decided to make a Canadian tour after his illness in 1921 because of the tributes that had come his way from Canada, Mrs. King was quite upset and did not encourage the idea. Even at his death, this possessive nature continued; she insisted that his body be buried in New Canaan. Carman's family finally had to obtain the aid of the Canadian government to convince Mrs. King of Carman's wish to be buried in Fredericton in the Forest Hill Cemetery overlooking the St. John River. A most interesting aspect of the personality of Mrs. King is revealed in a letter written by a relative of Carman's, a Mrs. Whitman, following the death of Carman in 1929.[5] In this letter, Mrs. Whitman, who was living in New Canaan when Carman died, tells of his death and the funeral there. She talks about the "great grief of the immediate blow" on Mrs. King; as the arrangements were being made, she realized "for the first time the hatred that existed between the King and Carman families." The Carman family, of course, found the whole relationship between the two quite unsavory, and disliked Mrs. King because of her dramatics and because they felt she had taken Carman away from those who loved him. Mrs. Whitman goes on to say: "Then, too, I realized how people behave in England and Canada when a famous person dies. Mrs. King, crushed by grief, never realized." Charles G. D. Roberts, Lorne Pierce, Carman's literary executor, and other Canadians, came to the funeral in New Canaan, but no arrangements were made for them "through thoughtlessness, largely because Mrs. King was so completely stunned," continues Mrs. Whitman. Perhaps this was more than a patroness grieving over a friend's death, but Mrs. King could obviously think of things only in terms of herself, not of others. Her grief was obviously very deep, yet she was able to continue her role as an exponent of "personal harmonizing," for "the service was very beautiful, Mrs. King would see to that." Mrs. Whitman makes another personal comment, too, when she says that Mrs. King, "after asking my advice, saying 'I do not wish to be bizarre. I am not his widow,' came in the deepest of crepe, simply swathed in it." She took again the opportunity to dramatize a situation. For Mrs. Whitman however, there was also the sense of tragic loss for Mrs. King, for she ends her letter with "Of course, her life henceforth must be a complete blank. It was Bliss who gave her all the spiritual values. Dr. King is simply an impossible money-maker."

The dramatics continued, too, when she came, with her husband, to Fredericton in the following September for the burial there. She carried the ashes in an urn on her lap, wearing the deepest mourning, originally designed for the occasion by a New York couturier. Her behavior was eventually embarrassing to all those concerned; she played the tragic figure well. Those who attended the ceremony in Christ Church Cathedral and at the interment remember Mrs. King as a statuesque figure, moaning into her black veil, quite overcome by emotion, with her husband, silent and taciturn at her side.

Dr. King was, after all, "an impossible money-maker," and he did not intervene in the relationship between his wife and Carman. He did not because there was nothing more to it than a deep friendship; Dr. King was not a stupid man. He was not too happy about the memory of the relationship, however. Lorne Pierce says that Dr. King did "not wish to be bothered about the Carman copyright [that had been left to Mrs. King by Carman]. He was anxious to be rid of it all—meaning the Carman papers lying about." [6] Years later, when Dr. King was asked his opinion of Carman, he thought for a minute and said, "He was a wart." It ended up that what bothered Dr. King most about Carman was that King would come home from a busy day and there would be Carman sitting in the best wicker chair by the open fire, with a rug thrown over his lap, and a drink held in his hand.[7] This is the remark of a man who saw Carman more as an opportunist than as a sharer of his wife's affections. There are things, however, which intensify the spiritual side of the relationship between Carman and Mrs. King. They had little personal names for each other; he called her "Star" and "April," both words which are prominent controlling images in his poetry, images which speak of fulfillment, contentment, heightened beauty. She was, however, a little less appealing in her nickname for him; to her "Blissikins" she was instead "April, dear heart." This, however, is modified in his endearment to his sister, Nancy, where the salutation is to "Nancy, dear heart" from "Blisskies." [8]

The friendship was intensified by the exchange of silver crucifixes. Carman always wore his when he was in her presence, and when he was away from her he wore it secretly under his clothing. He did not want to have to explain his relationship with her, and he was embarrassed when anyone would ask questions that he thought were too personal about their friendship. He was always loyal to her and he would not listen to any cruel remarks that were made about her. She was severely criticized for over-acting her role in his life, and often cutting remarks were made about her strange ideas. Once when she was criticized for the rather trite aspect of her philosophy of beauty, truth, and goodness, Carman sprang to her defense with strong language. Mrs. King arranged quite dramatically that her crucifix be given to Lorne Pierce after her death.[9] She had put the cross in a dove-colored cloth bag, handed it to her secretary, and asked that it be given to Pierce on her death. The crosses commemorate the great affection they had for one another, and they intensify the purity of their relationship; it was a strong spiritual relationship controlled by a woman who enjoyed her role of patron and friend over a man who demanded that people shelter him and guide him in many directions.

Much has been made of Carman's friendship with Mrs. King. Subtle innuendoes accompany any criticism of his poetry where

Mrs. King's name is mentioned.[10] The myth about Carman suggests that there was a strong love relationship between the two. In Fredericton, many of the people who remember Carman snicker when the two names are put together. There was, I feel, no more to it than what it appeared to be. The myth suggests that perhaps a relationship faintly touched with the sordid enhances the poet's reputation. It does nothing for Carman, just as the search that some critics have made for the "lost lover" of the earlier poems does nothing for his poetry. Mrs. King was very important to Carman. She encouraged him when he needed encouragement; she fed him and clothed him. Often she suggested topics for poems. She liked to edit his verse but he paid little attention to her criticism. She was a very important person in his personal life, but to exaggerate the meaning of their relationship only to enlarge upon the myth, to enhance what is an extremely ordinary and often dull life, is to be dishonest about Carman. He was not capable of having an illicit relationship; it would not have been his nature to keep it secret. He told everything, often too many times. We cannot assume that this secret was a secret at all. The relationship was what it appeared to be: a strong friendship based on similar tastes, ideas, and a mutual need for companionship, and understanding.

Friendship was the strongest guiding force in Carman's life. His papers are full of personal cards and letters; he retained anything that was a show of friendship. He wrote many letters and always answered quickly any letter that was written to him. He enjoyed, too, the role of the poet which he coupled with his ideas of friendship as the stronger factors in his life. He continued to add many masks to his behavior. He was particularly proud of his flowing hair which he had let grow long while he was at Harvard. In a sense, it almost became a fetish with him; he was very careful who he had to cut it, and spent hours on it. He added to this image of himself other things which he thought would intensify the picture that his contemporaries had of him. He wanted to be "tragic and Greek." Often, perhaps, he spent more time creating the picture of a poet as he thought it should be, than in working over poems that would prove that he was a poet. After he met Mary Perry King, he added a large Stetson hat and full-flowing cravat. Soon after came the heavy tweeds and hand-made sandal type shoes.

About 1910 he started to wear rings and bracelets set in silver and turquoise. Today this would be thought effeminate; in Carman's day it was the acceptable and predictable eccentricity of a poet. He was always at ease in his clothes, and those who met him were overwhelmed by his charm and tender kindness. With his friends he was very much at ease, showing proof that he was at home in the life that he had created for himself; that life for him was rich and full.

He was not, however, at home when reading before an audience. After a severe illness in 1920 at Saranac Lake in the Adirondacks, there was a benefit for him in Toronto organized by Siegfried Sassoon, and he received many letters from Canadians who wished him good health. He was so touched by this display of affection that from then on he made frequent visits to his native country. People who heard him speak remark about his poor stage manner, bad voice, and aloofness at receptions; others have ascribed this manner to supreme shyness, but it could be another mask. He was given the LL.D. by the University of New Brunswick and McGill University, and the Litt.D. by Trinity College in Hartford. He was elected a Corresponding Member of the Royal Society of Canada, and in 1928 received the Lorne Pierce Medal of the Royal Society of Canada for his distinguished contribution to letters. He was honored, too, by the American Academy of Arts and Letters, and awarded posthumously the medal of the Poetry Society of America. In the year before his death, he went on a tour of Canada through to Vancouver and down to California. He died suddenly in New Canaan on Sunday, June 8, 1929.

Canada wanted to respect his wish to be buried in Fredericton, and after the funeral service in New Canaan his ashes were returned to Fredericton where a state burial took place. On October 18, a granite tombstone, designed by Carman himself and Mrs. King, was unveiled by the premier of New Brunswick, J. B. M. Baxter. Twenty-five years after his death, representatives of the University of New Brunswick planted a scarlet maple tree at his grave. It was a morning ceremony after a night of heavy rain and dramatically and romantically the sun broke through as the service began. It was one way for Canada, for the University of New Brunswick and for Fredericton particularly, to acknowledge a favorite son and to grant the wish expressed in one of his poems:

Mask and Myth

Let me have a scarlet maple
For the grave-tree at my head,
With the quiet sun behind it,
In the years when I am dead.
                    ("The Grave-Tree")

But the centenary of Carman's birth, 1961, passed almost completely unnoticed in the world of Canadian letters. His reputation was then and continues to be at one of its lowest points; it is obvious that he will never regain the reputation he held at the beginning of the twentieth-century. The reasons for this neglect are various; only a few poems, but many separate lines and stanzas, are worthy of remembrance; his prose is almost impossible. Bliss Carman continues to be an ambiguous figure and poet. The legend and the myth, the facts and the pose, play against each other to weave a rich complex of meaning into the life of Bliss Carman. Sufficient paradox can be read into the life of any person, particularly a famous one, and what stands out most prominently in Carman's life and works is the contradiction.

The most obvious quality about him is the mask which he put on his own person, his own life, his own role as a writer. He affected a pose, and so much enjoyed it that eventually even he was unable to distinguish between the mask he put on for others and his true self. Is it any wonder, then, that there are so many interpretations of Carman as a writer, that so many myths appear, that local loyalty in a sense has destroyed the clear picture of one of Canada's best nineteenth-century poets? Here was a man so steeped in tradition, so susceptible to external influences, that he never came forth as a separate individual.

What remains is a combination of the legends about his life, and the masks he self-consciously wore. Behind these two things there appears to be nothing original and fresh, either in the work he produced, or the relationships he cherished. The myth and the mask have to stand strong and alone, because there is no man behind them. There was someone who had a high ability at assimilation, who was able to put together in quite a logical order all the influences upon him into a fragmented impression. Total integration of assimilation is not present; it could not be so. Carman was so much a product of his time, of the tradition-loving Freder-

iction of the nineteenth-century, of an educational system satu-
rated in the use of models and the past, that he could not turn out
any other way. But, he is worthy of study as a poet because he
does show how tradition can produce a poet whose work occasionally rises to heights of greatness. His lyrical gift, acquired and
not innate, is not surpassed by his Canadian contemporaries.

The work of Bliss Carman demonstrates the falsity of the idea
that art is self-expression pure and simple, that a poet's work is the
transcript of his own personal feeling and experiences. It proves,
rather, that poetry is more than a simple embodiment of experience and is determined by convention and by literary tradition.
Carman does give his reader his own views and experiences, but
they are always views and experiences brought to him by others.
During his life he was never in control; he always wanted to have
someone else in control for him. Perhaps he was not capable of an
original thought; perhaps he was merely a "daisy picker." But he
was able to express himself in a world where few people can, and
even though the thought may not be new, the form old and often
trite, Carman had a wonderful ability to communicate what
meaning the world held for him.

So Carman's poetry moves in various streams: the poetry that
expresses the world as he wishes it to be, his dream world; the
poetry that is the 'mask,' the poetry that he knew people wanted
and expected him to write; and the poetry that serves as his escape from both the world of reality and the world of mask, which
for Carman are not distinguishable. For Carman there was no
reality; reality for him was what the world may be, what it once
was, what it could be. Even when he disparaged his contemporary world, it was those things in it that could lead to destruction. So the numerous masks melt into one another, the world of
reality is not distinguished, and the legends are born, out of which
come the myths developed by people who could not find an answer to the question "who is Bliss Carman?"

There is no real conclusion as to what Carman is, what he
writes, what his tenets were. He obviously never knew himself,
and that was because he wore too many masks for the people who
knew him. Lorne Pierce says that Carman is a minor poet, and
implies that the man himself was greater than his works.[11] Even in
his correspondence with famous people—Conrad, Kipling, Santa-

yana and others—this is not evidenced. The world of repeated phrases and platitudes appears again. There is no man behind the masks, and the legends, and the myths.

Carman's work and his life became for him a kind of convention; both were masks yet they were so because he had made himself a product of his own experience. And biography does not help to recreate Carman's art; it serves, rather, to help us understand it. With Carman it never makes any difference really to know when a poem was written, what had produced the poem in his mind. His poetry remains wonderfully static, and in him it is a virtue. The poetry of Bliss Carman proves Lionel Trilling's point, however, that the pastness of a work is often part of its meaning and value. Carman's life was uninspiring, and no amount of conjecture can make it interesting. But what his life was, what he produced during it, is all part of the meaning of his work. There are the masks he put on for the sake of others, and the ones he put on for himself; there are the myths created by the public. Behind them all is a man who is part and parcel of them. With his poetry before us, these impressions present a new dimension in seeing Carman's role as a Canadian poet.

CHAPTER 3

Performance

B LISS CARMAN himself was able to recognize the value and quality of his own work. In a letter to his sister, written in 1892, after a few broadsheets of his poems had been printed privately and a few verses had been published, a year before his first volume of poems came out, he said:

Old Nature lies out there in the sun, all so beautiful and fair; and poetry is what she would say if she could speak. No, we are all only poor children, mortal children; and with great difficulty we try to make ourselves understood to one another. Yet we cannot. No heart can speak to any other heart; but every heart has its own sorrow and joy alone—quite alone. But poets, real poets, are those who come nearest to being able to speak. . . . Now . . . may I ever be preserved from a false estimate of my little verses. They are too sorry and doleful and too intimately private to be great or good poetry.[1]

And he was right. It is not great or good poetry, but there are a few poems which "come nearest to being able to speak"; it is nature which concerns him most, a view of nature that he, "with great difficulty," tried to communicate to others.

Though he attempted to do these things, he knew his own limitations; he knew he could not be original, and thus he became an imitator. Originality and freshness gave to others; theirs was the "task for a summer's day." [2]

To be fresh, to be original, to be conclusive, to be untrite and compelling, yet to be alluring and convincing and seductive also; to astonish and overcome and carry wholly away, yet never to antagonize nor offend [3]

was not his task.

It is for this reason that his first volume of poetry is his most outstanding; it is the product of the years of apprenticeship during which poems were written for various occasions, produced under the influence that was affecting him most at the time. He had printed a few poems privately, in broadsheets that he sent to friends, and some of his poems had been printed in prominent magazines of the day, *The Atlantic Monthly* being the most reputable. In 1893, his first volume appeared, *Low Tide on Grand Pré: A Book of Lyrics,* and it established Carman's reputation; it was a volume of verse that showed all of Carman's interest, for its themes and forms were to be followed, sometimes with greater intensity, in the volumes of poetry to follow. It shows Carman at his best; it reveals, too, that Carman is a poet who does not gradually develop after his first volume of poetry is published. He had found what he wanted to say, and he continued to say it. Many poets, such as Yeats, show great development as they grow older; Carman was thirty-two when *Low Tide on Grand Pré* was printed and except for occasional bursts of imagination, his poetry remained the same in mood and intensity.

James Cappon, in his book on Carman, considers the title poem "too slight an effort to be called a masterpiece." [4] Undoubtedly, Cappon was disturbed by the word "masterpiece," which is, admittedly, used too often in reviews and on book covers, for he goes on to say that the poem is "an unforgettable addition to the stock of fine Canadian lyrics." [5] Cappon is refusing to face his responsibility to the poem in this kind of statement; too often critics of Canadian verse excuse their remarks by putting the poetry they are examining into a Canadian framework and thus excusing it for its limitations. As lyric, and as a representative poem of its time, Canadian and otherwise, "Low Tide on Grand Pré" holds a strong and high position. Here is Carman at his best as far as technique is concerned; the five-line stanzas are finely wrought, the rhythm beautifully executed. This technical facility explains why Peter McArthur talks of Carman reciting his poems to an audience that "vibrated to his rhythms." [6] This is probably a reference to the *Vagabondia* poems that were to come next, but the rhythm of "Low Tide on Grand Pré," though quieter, has a vitality about it that is always with Carman:[7]

> There down along the elms at dusk
> We lifted dripping blade to drift,

Through twilight scented fine like musk,
Where night and gloom awhile uplift,
Nor sunder soul and soul adrift.

The meaning of this poem is usually related to one of the legends that surrounds Carman's life and for which there is little proof. The poem obviously expresses the poet's longing for a lost love, for another time that can be no more; he compares his grief on the loss of the girl he loves to the movement of the tide on the river. Some critics go so far as to mention the name of the woman Carman is talking about.[8] There is another interpretation which seems more valid, however. The poem was written in its final draft in 1887, the year after Carman's mother died. Her death had been the largest crisis of his life, and the poem quite dramatically is concerned with the death of a loved one rather than with a lover who is gone and a love affair of another time. The love affair interpretation is based on the fourth and seventh stanzas:

Was it a year or lives ago
We took the grasses in our hands,
And caught the summer flying low
Over the waving meadow lands,
And held it there between our hands?
. . . .
And that we took into our hands
Spirit of life or subtler thing—
Breathed on us there, and loosed the bands
Of death, and taught us, whispering,
The secrets of some wonder-thing.

This last stanza, however, leads into the stanza where the idea of death is the main factor, and is contrasted to the "spirit of life":

Then all your face grew light, and seemed
To hold the shadow of the sun;
The evening faltered, and I deemed
That time was ripe, and years had done
Their wheeling underneath the sun.

These last two lines refer to death itself—life for someone is over, a life that was "ripe"; this is no reference to a young girl, but to someone whose life has been lived. When, in the ninth stanza, he speaks of "keen delight," it is the joy of knowing each other and the learning acquired, not the overpowering joy of a sexual relationship; this is a love based on a deeper and more spiritual basis. This concept is reinforced in the third stanza of the poem where he speaks of "one beloved face . . . / So long from home," and "home" connotes hearth and mother. Carman's mother had spent much time with Carman and the Roberts family on the summer vacations; it is not surprising that he should write of missing her during the first summer spent on the Grand Pré since her death. He remembers when all her "face grew light, and seemed/ To hold the shadow of the sun."

The poem does support various interpretations, and most critics lean toward the one of the lost lover. It seems, however, that the initial poem in this volume shows two facets of Carman's creative ability which were to stay with him all his life: he created a poem which expressed what he personally felt about some real experience in his life, and at the same time suggested what he thought others would expect; his work was always conditioned by what Carman interpreted as the prevailing taste of the reading public at the time he was writing. Young poets, in their first volumes, are supposed to write of anguish and pain, of lost loves and heartache. This duality of purpose creates the double theme; all readers can agree that he is talking of someone who has gone, but various interpretations can be produced as to who that someone is. This vagueness is not purposeful; Carman thought he was clear enough, but he was aware that the aspect was diffuse. So, this poem shows his own intoxication with words, with the unusual image ("we caught the summer flying low"), and because of this intoxication with *how* things are said, he often forgot what he was saying. Carman never did learn when to discard, when to save an idea for another poem; he packed his poems with so many images, colors, and ideas—often even with extra stanzas—that the vagueness persists through nearly all his work. It is especially evident in the title poem of *Low Tide on Grand Pré*. This poem would have been better if it had been broken into two poems, or tied together at the end with a cogent meaning. He could have spoken of a lost loved one, used two examples of a sweetheart and his mother, and then resolved the poem with a universal statement on personal loss. To end the way he does is dramatic, and has a nice poetic quality, but what does it really say thematically?

> The night has fallen, and the tide . . .
> Now and again comes drifting home,
> Across these aching barrens wide,
> A sigh like driven wind or foam:
> In grief the flood is bursting home.

This tendency of Carman's to looseness in both structure and theme is evidenced in other poems in this volume, particularly in "Pulvis et Umbra." Here is Carman's imagination floating in many directions, guided in part by the influence of Poe's "The Raven." Though the "Nevermore" of the raven is not heard, the night-moth's visits to the study in a lonely cottage by the sea manage to convey a special atmosphere and a strong sense of place. Unfortunately it takes Carman too long to give Poe's "indefinite suggestiveness of meaning"; often it seems that, for Carman, Poe's "indefinite" applies only to the number of stanzas. Within five verses the mood is conveyed, but Carman does not seem sure of what it is, so that the poem becomes repetitive.

Some poets can use repetition successfully for emphasis; for Carman it becomes merely redundant:

> For man walks the world with mourning
>   Down to death, and leaves no trace,
> With the dust upon his forehead,
>   And the shadow in his face.

With a minor variation, this stanza later becomes:

> For man walks the world in Twilight,
>   But the morn shall wipe all trace
> Of the dust from off his forehead,
>   And the shadow from his face.

Where many poets show a tendency to slough off an influence, Carman seems to clutch it closer to his poetic heart. In this volume, Poe is the prominent influence; it is as if Carman were trying to make sure he had captured the essence of the master of mood;

at times he is not sure and so repeats himself. There is emotion that is diffuse, a situation that is vague, a bereavement that is undefined yet repeated—as in the theme of "Where the Guelder Roses Bloom":

> When the Guelder roses blow,
> Love that dies so long ago,
>
> Why wilt thou return so oft,
> With that whisper sad and soft
>
> On thy pleading lips again,
> "Guendolen, Guendolen."

Guendolen becomes the lost figure in many of the poems in this volume, and she is coupled with ghostly nights, stars, shadows and silence. A few stanzas from "A Northern Vigil" echo Poe again:

> Come, for the night is cold,
> The ghostly moonlight fills
> Hollow and rift and fold
> Of the eerie Ardise hills!
>
> The windows of my room
> Are dark with bitter frost,
> The stillness aches with doom
> Of something loved and lost.
>
> Outside, the great blue star
> Burns in the ghostland pale,
> Where giant Algebar
> Holds on the endless trail.

This atmosphere is continued in the next poem in the volume, "The Eavesdropper," but for a moment the reader is fooled into thinking that perhaps a new dimension will emerge, that of a strong sensual emotion:

> In a still room at hush of dawn,
> My Love and I lay side by side

> And heard the roaming forest wind
> Stir in the paling autumn-tide.

But this is not to be continued; the Poe mystery comes back, and the reality is lost:

> Then as the purple twilight came
> And touched the vines along our eaves,
> Another shadow stood without
> And gloomed the dancing of the leaves.
>
> . . . .
> I saw retreating on the hills
> Looming and sinister and black,
> The stealthy figure swift and huge
> Of One who strode and looked not back.

"The Eavesdropper" does, however, suggest a strain in Carman that he was to develop as he grew older: a capacity for description in nature not colored by dilated emotion:

> Outside, a yellow maple tree,
> Shifting upon the silvery blue
> With tiny multitudinous sound,
> Rustled to let the sunlight through.

Here is the world of reality. Carman attempts to describe only in fresh terms; he becomes the poet able to say in words what his reader may have felt but been unable to express. The poem becomes a simple, lyrical statement.

He can also merge a kind of transcendental philosophy with his description of nature and his place in it, so that the reality of the picture mingles with, rather than is hidden by, the thematic statement. In "A Windflower" the description is only rarely repetitive, and the simplicity of the pantheistic philosophy does not mar the poem's effect; it does, in fact, create a unity, a fusing of form and theme which few of the poems in this volume do have:

> Between the roadside and the wood,
> Between the dawning and the dew,

A tiny flower before the sun,
Ephemeral in time, I grew.

. . . .

But down the dayspan of the year
The feet of straying winds came by;
And all my trembling soul was thrilled
To follow one lost mountain cry.

. . . .

Tonight can bring no healing now;
The calm of yesternight is gone;
Surely the wind is but the wind,
And I a broken waif thereon.

This, too, is a shorter poem than the majority of poems in this volume, which generally tend to become monotonous and reveal all of Carman's bad aspects as a poet and as a person. When he decides not to repeat himself because the philosophy is not clear or because he is trying for Poesque vagueness, Carman becomes a better poet. The lyric quality is at its best, the images are good, the statement is not diluted.

Three two-stanza poems, "The Unreturning," "A Sea-Drift" and "A Sea Child" are the best in this volume. Gone is melancholy that is weird and mysterious; instead, it is merely pensive. There is a reality to the poems in both theme and image. Artificial devices borrowed from others are not repeated in order to bring them to the reader's attention; rather, the image-clusters form a descriptive pattern in their originality. Carman was to develop this range of the fresh image in his later poems, and to culminate this imagery in the short lyrics and odes. In "A Sea-Drift" he compares desire to "the meadow-birds at dawn" that "Haunt the spaces of the rain." Though he seems to dote on comparison, it is the actual description, without a metaphor or simile, that creates the best poetry. In "The Unreturning" he uses the device of a young poet in piling adjectives one on the other, as in "old eternal spring," "sad eternal way," and "tender rosy light," and there is little to distinguish the poem except in its culminating effect. In "A Sea Child," the prevailing image is clear and not too precious; he uses strong words to give vigor and intensity to his rhythms:

The lover of child Marjory
Had one white hour of life brim full;

Now the old nurse, the rocking sea,
Hath him to lull.

The daughter of child Marjory
Hath in her veins, to beat and run,
The glad indomitable sea,
The strong white sun.

But though the images at times are forceful and clear, the philosophy is too mystical to be clear; he relies too heavily on suggestion to convey meaning and for this reason the meaning does not become clear. The philosophy does become more evident when he relates the mysteries of life to the seasons, especially to spring. The spring songs were to become a characteristic feature of his verse in the years to come. He is interested in the seasons in all their aspects in this volume, and equates the cycle with the high and low moments in the pulse of man. He takes the ordinary view, associating winter with death and coldness of emotions, autumn with the ending of life and with nostalgia, summer with the glorious moments that show completion, and spring with moments of awakening and beginnings. He uses the outward manifestations of spring, the movements of wild animals, the coming from the south of the birds, the growth of plants, the running of the sap in the maple trees, the budding of the leaves. Spring is that moment when man can renew himself and learn of what he truly is and what he will become, as in "The Pensioners":

Until her April train goes by,
And then because we are the kin
Of every hill flower on the hill
We must arise and walk therein.

The rhythm here is a little too pat, the expression a little too trite, but it points toward his concept of man; there is mystery still in the cosmic call to man and nature in the spring, and it serves Carman as a predominant image, one with which he could associate easily. Fredericton is a place where spring is felt so obviously —heard in the crack-up of the St. John River and smelled in the greenery of the elms on spring evenings—and Carman was deeply aware of the senses and their reaction to nature. April, too, was the month of his birth, and he had a mystical attachment to that season of the year. It was the time when people came home, when man learned the true meaning of existence; it was, as in "Afoot," the time of year for mystical callings and yearnings, and beginnings:

> On the frontier of desire
> I will drink the last regret,
> And then forth beyond the morrow
> Where I may but half forget.
>
> . . . .
>
> And the Mother there once more
> Will rewhisper her dark word,
> That my brothers all may wonder,
> Hearing then as once I heard.
>
> . . . .
>
> And though I be far away,
> When the early violets come
> Smiling at the door with April,
> Say, "The vagabonds are home!"

The whole volume introduces the themes which were to continue throughout Carman's career; it shows, too, the beginning of a lack of resolution in his poetry. April is the moment of a beginning, and other times it is "the cruelest month"; the wind has an important transcendental meaning but at other times "surely the wind is but the wind"; the cycle of nature is predominant in meaning yet at times it is replete with ambiguities. There are the three main images which occur and reoccur throughout the rest of his work: the wind, nature as seen in the growth of the flower, any flower, and April as a turning point in the year.

The wind, for Carman, is more than a physical phenomenon, constantly rising and falling and blending; Carman looks beyond its actual presence into the invisible forces that propel it, into the invisible life it breathes. He associates it with life and death and searches for the reasons why it does not give notice as to when it will come. He searches the ambivalence of the wind; he sees it bring a "spring rain," and he sees it bring destruction. Because it does not warn of its coming, and because man cannot predict it, the wind for Carman becomes a meaningful symbol, as it reflects the conflicts and ambiguities of life. As a symbol, the wind is not tangible like the landscape, a maple tree, a bird, yet it is part of all these. It comes from places unknown and goes to places unseen. For Carman it is beyond life and is, as it was for Duncan Campbell Scott, his contemporary, a "sign of the spirit." [10]

Though Carman often sees the wind through mystical eyes, his main associations with it, of regeneration, destruction, immense power and unpredictability, are part of the Christian tradition to which the poet belongs. He may, at times, move outside into an occult philosophy, but the roots are basically Christian, embedded in *The Book of Common Prayer*. The wind in its transcendent power becomes a symbol of the power of God. In the first creation the wind is part of the generative force of God; it becomes, too, a symbol of the destructive powers, and the fall of man from the state of innocence to knowledge of good and evil. The wind is a guide to the infinite reality of life. And Carman, like a child, learns of the wind; he is a "broken waif" of the wind, but he becomes a "harpstring of the wind." This volume of poetry, *Low Tide on Grand Pré*, shows Carman thinking and questioning the wind; it is primarily a physical experience as he describes it, but it becomes more than that. The elements of the unknown and unpredictable make the wind a symbol of mystery and transcendence. It is aligned with discovery of the ultimate meaning of life.

In *Low Tide on Grand Pré* Carman is concerned primarily with this search. As a group, the poems and their subjects allow for the expression of this search. Common emotions are examined by and for people who are minutely aware of the eternal cycle of birth and death around them. This is an elemental relationship with nature, a nature that cannot be understood completely or harnessed in any way, or predicted as to specific direction. In most of the poems there is the suggestion of the presence of a guiding power, something which controls nature, man, and life. The cycle becomes a primary form for Carman, here, and in all his poetry. The world of nature and man depends for its existence upon a series of complex and interlocking cyclic actions. The ebb of the tide is only one portion of nature's water cycle. Man's life is in itself a self-resolving circle, dependent upon the vitality of the person involved. Though things die and change, there is a never-ending process of generic rebirth as steady as the sun's wheeling circuit through the sky, or the seasons' relentless progression. The cycle for Carman never loses its sense of mystery and awe, but reveals a way of life filled with the joy of natural harmony, progressive and static. The whole world is a fascination; it reveals so many things to the poet, of the world, and of man:

> We shall lie down and hear the frost
>   Walk in the dead leaves restlessly,
> Or somewhere on the iron coast
>   Learn the oblivion of the sea.
>
> It matters not. And yet I dream
>   Of dreams fulfilled and rest somewhere
> Before this restless heart is stilled
>   And all its fancies blown to air.
>   ("The Vagabonds")

Low Tide on Grand Pré, in 1893, and *Behind the Arras,* in 1895, show Carman doing what he liked best to do. They were not too popular with the public, however; his fame came with poems he wrote for a public that wanted light and easy verse. He pictured a public yearning for young and attractive poets writing easy songs about a normal life; he gave them what he thought they wanted. He was right; his reputation became wide overnight. It was again an example of Carman doing what he thought others would want, and not doing what he really wanted to do himself. Three volumes express this direction: *Songs From Vagabondia,* 1894; *More Songs From Vagabondia,* 1896; and *Last Songs From Vagabondia,* 1900; all were written in collaboration with Richard Hovey and are commonly called the *Vagabondia* series.

Hovey and Carman had become fast friends, and both had deserted other fields to accept the challenge of poetry.[11] They had decided to set a framework for poetry and poets in America; they wanted to direct the attention of readers and critics alike to the new movements in poetry written in North America and away from the respect and attention paid to poets living in England. They had to create a supply for the public demand in order to captivate an audience. In order to gain this audience, they felt that they should deal with lighter subjects; they chose a lyrical pattern that would be easy to remember; they hoped to add to the number of readers of poetry in America. So they followed a pattern often used by young poets. A light, Bohemian quality is the trademark of this verse, mingled with a little satire, a great deal of humor, happy love lyrics, and the occasional search for a higher plane through mystical symbolism. In these volumes Carman seems to raise himself from the melancholy that marks his earlier —and his later—poetry. The lighter poems in the *Vagabondia* series suggest a strong contrast to the other Carman and present the question of sincerity as part of the poet's direction. Careful examination of the volumes shows, however, that the poems of Carman, for the most part, tend to be tinged with his deeper philosophy and melancholy. The volumes comprise the final printing of poems usually published before in the various magazines by which Hovey and Carman had supported themselves. They show little or no organization or grouping as to theme or form, and are undoubtedly the least effective collection of poetry of one poet— let alone two—ever to come upon the literary scene. There is a total lack of discrimination in these volumes; they read like ramblings about no specific question; they have no core or circumference which holds them together.

It is natural, perhaps, that the volumes should turn out this way. The poems had been written for the pages of popular magazines of the day, magazines with wide circulations appealing to the greater mass of the population; therefore the tone is ordinary and the emotions appealed to, too average. It is unfortunate that Carman's need to support himself financially through his poetry did not cause him to direct his verse to more universal statement. He looked down upon the readers of these magazines and consequently produced poetry trite in manner, unsophisticated in fashion. This was a time when he could have taken his bent toward Wordsworth, or his affinity for Housman, and produced a nicely lyrical poetry with a universal appeal.

And so, a kind of Bohemian spirit emerges, but only in the way that Carman reads the Bohemian spirit. It is another example of his aiming for a certain condition, a certain pose, and missing the target. He does not quite make it so many times either because he did not have the intelligence, or because he could not see into the "heart of things." His Bohemianism is artificial; the whole aura is of a studied casualness. He does taunt the conventional world, the desire for material things and the need for more money. He ridicules the American dream of success, but only in the slightest of ways. His world of "vagabondia" is one in which a person is freed of the social restraints and gains satisfaction from the natural world around him; it is a kind of return to nature, but there is nothing complete in it. Carman was incapable of hostility, a trait essential in a true Bohemian. Though he condemns the hold the world has on the individual, there is no revolt in his voice. There is a touch of Whitman in Carman's feeling that the values of the individual are submerged in the social world, and that there are times to get away. But it is obvious that he only wanted to get away for a little while.

It is Hovey who sets the tone of the books; for him it is "Off with the fetters/ that chafe and restrain," while Carman talks of "The Joys of the Road," interested mainly in the variety of nature that he finds about him. His poetry becomes more a picture of the landscape than a statement of philosophy. When he does deal with his ideas of living, he becomes quite horrible. In "Spring Song" he says:

> Shrilling pipe or fluting whistle,
> In the valleys come again;
> Fife of frog and call of tree-toad,
> All my brothers, five or three-toed,
> With their revel no more vetoed,
> Making music in the rain;

This is the worst of the *Vagabondia* poems, and is by far the worst poem that Carman had published. The rhyme in the stanza quoted is atrocious; the image "All my brothers, five or three-toed" is infantile; the idea as well as the contrast is very bad. The opening lines, "Make me over, mother April/ When the sap begins to stir," makes a reader admit that some "sap" is stirring, all right. The last stanza of the poem commits every poetic blunder; it has no style at all, no good figure of speech, very bad rhyme, and the idea is repulsive:

> Only make me over, April,
> When the sap begins to stir!
> Make me man or make me woman,

> Make me oaf or ape or human,
> Cup of flower, or cone of fir;
> Make me anything but neuter
> When the sap begins to stir.

The poem is Carman at his awkward worst; both structure and idea are wretched.[12]

There are times in this volume, however, when Carman does attain a fine lyrical quality with a light tone; in "In the House of Idiedaily" the first lines have a special piquancy:

> Oh, but life went gayly, gayly,
> In the house of Idiedaily!

Cappon uses the word "naïve" to describe this poem,[13] and the word suggests the special quality of Carman's *Vagabondia* poems. There is naïveté here, a lack of sophistication, an unaffected ingenuousness which marks the smaller lyrics. Again, it is the Housman touch in "The Marching Morrows":

> Now gird thee well for courage,
> My knight of twenty year
> Against the marching morrows
> That fill the world with fear!

This naïve quality is present when he tries for humor, as in "The Two Bobbies":

> Bobbie Burns and Bobbie Browning,
> They're the boys I'd like to see.
> Though I'm not the boy for Bobbie,
> Bobbie is the boy for me.

He mixes this naïveté with a kind of carelessness, which gives the poems an authentic quality of spontaneity. As he said to H. D. C. Lee: "The note in the Vagabondias is careless but never flippant. It sometimes treats deep things lightly, but that is only on the surface ripple." [14] He wanted always to be taken seriously.

This note, and its accompanying question of the sincerity of approach—since there are three volumes in this series—rings

quite strongly in the last two volumes. In *More Songs From Vagabondia* this note is struck most particularly in "In a Garden":

> Thought is a garden wide and old
> For airy creatures to explore,
> Where grow the great fantastic flowers
> With truth for honey at the core.
>
> There like a wild marauding bee
> Made desperate by hungry fears,
> From gorgeous *If* to dark *Perhaps*
> I blunder down the dusk of years.

Here Carman is dealing with a serious question, and the image
does control the poem; with some imagination a reader can see
the cleverness of the statement and comment on the meaning. The
poem is not, however, very clear. H. D. C. Lee, who had written a
doctoral dissertation on Carman for the Université de Rennes,
had asked Carman about the meaning of some of the images in
his work. In a letter to Lee, Carman tried to explain the images
for "they might mean the writer's instinctive sense of
supersenses." [15] He admits that in his early work he often used
images that are not clear, and then goes on to say:

> But that does not mean the work is insincere, simply because it has
> no lucid meaning or interpretation. It simply means that the young
> poet is so carried away by the stress of his own imagination and of his
> rapture in rhythm and sound, that he permits himself to wander into
> the vague regions of suggestion. He overemphasizes the need of hyp-
> notic power in poetry and does not realize the need for common-sense.
> I have written many lines that have no sense, it appears, but I never
> deliberately meant to defraud or fool my possible readers. And of
> course in the later work this blemish is quite outgrown. [16]

Carman was aware that his work was often criticized for its insin-
cerity, a censure applied because frequently he was so carried
away by his method of saying something that he forgot the
thought that controls the images. He became intoxicated with his
own poetry too frequently, especially in the *Vagabondia* series.
Admittedly there is spirit in these poems, a good fancy at work;

but the lines become extravagant and at times are mere fluff with little or no meaning underneath.

When he is conscious of his theme, he assumes the role of a teacher. Didacticism is always a strong part of Carman's verse, but it is always apparent; when he has something serious to say he does not shroud his idea with the fine use of language often established in his lighter verse; rather, he often tries to be deliberately unpoetic when he feels that he has a strong message for his reader. In the *Vagabondia* series he frequently sermonizes on the natural world and what it offers to man. The message becomes banal, as in "The Mendicants":

> But there be others, happier few,
> The vagabondish sons of God,
> Who know the by-ways and the flowers,
> And care not how the world may plod.
>
> They idle down the traffic lanes,
> And loiter through the woods with spring;
> To them the glory of the earth,
> Is but to hear a bluebird sing.

Often he uses allegory to illustrate his ideas, as any good preacher would; more often than not, however, the allegory only limps along.

The important accomplishment of the *Vagabondia* series is the variety that both poets reveal. Hovey, too, varies form and concept, but he does not have Carman's lightness. *Vagabondia* was Hovey's idea, but Carman expresses its grace and fancy in a far more effective fashion. There is, however, more fire in Hovey's verses; he has the vigor that the life of "vagabondia" demands, even though in his personal life he enjoyed luxuries and did not care too much for life on the open road. The friends created in the first two volumes of the *Vagabondia* series poetry of the good life, poetry marked by a youthful exuberance. There is an ease to the verse, a freedom in both content and style. But Hovey is the exuberant one, Carman the quiet mystic; the shadow of melancholy that marks all of Carman's poetry marks the books. The epitaph on his gravestone is on the opening cover and pages of *Songs From Vagabondia*:

[56]

> Have little care that life is brief,
> And less that art is long,
> Success is in the silences
> And Fame is in the song.

This melancholy marks the last volume of the *Vagabondia* series, and is even suggested in the title, *Last Songs From Vagabondia*.

The note of melancholy, always heard in Carman's verse, becomes dominant in the majority of his work done between 1895 and 1902. In this period he wrote many elegies and memorial verses to commemorate famous men and occasions in the past. Though some critics see this as a distinct compartment in Carman's poetic development,[17] it is not a new phase; it is, instead, an extension, predictable at that, of a tone established in his earlier verse. What does mark this verse is its lyrical quality; Carman was dealing with an emotion that he liked to dwell upon and it is no surprise that the form turns out to be among his most successful. The elegy freed Carman from the restraints of the mystical that he had put on his early verse. He takes the classical elegy, touches it with strong pastoral images, and produces a poetry that is easy to understand while being very much in fashion at that time. So this time he was writing poetry the public wanted and dealing with themes that were closer to his nature than the free "vagabondia" quality or the transcendental flavor established in his earlier work.

The poems in *By the Aurelian Wall and Other Elegies*, 1898, are marked again by an uneven quality, both as a group and as separate poems. In "A Seamark, a Threnody for Robert Louis Stevenson," Carman reveals the full range of his poetic capabilities; he can also create the devastatingly poor stanza,

> He "was not born for age." Ah no,
> For everlasting youth is his!
> Part of the lyric of the earth
> With spring and leaf and blade he is.

and yet end the poem with grace and an image of beauty:

> High on a peak adrift with mist,
> And round whose bases, far beneath

> The snow-white wheeling tropic birds,
> The emerald dragon breaks his teeth.

His elegies to Shelley and Keats are mentioned elsewhere in this book,[18] but in three other poems in this volume Carman reaches the widest dimension of his work as an elegist: "A Norse Child's Requiem," "In the Heart of the Hills," and "The Grave-Tree." Here he is not aiming for some cosmic statement, or for any imitation of the classics. Instead he is consciously fusing theme and form, producing his most integrated poetry up to this time. For a moment his lapses are gone; there is little confusion as to image development, no lack of unity in statement.

In ten quatrains, "A Norse Child's Requiem" unites simple statement with clear lyrical phraseology. Here Carman recognizes the truth of what he is examining; he does not elevate with lofty images a statement that does not demand it. Instead he gives the story of the Norse child a kind of clear poignancy that only simple statement will produce:

> Content thee, not with pity;
> Be solaced, not with tears;
> But when the whitethroats waken
> Through the revolving years.

Occasionally the rhythm is faulty and a few words out of place ("moiety," for example) but the overall effect is rarely equalled in Carman's verse:

> Then winter be thy housing,
> Thy lullaby the rain,
> Thou hero of no battle,
> Thou saint without a stain.

"In the Heart of the Hills" again shows Carman's affinity with Housman. He is obviously talking about the grave of someone close to him in the Forest Hills Graveyard in Fredericton, which is on the hills overlooking the St. John River:

> Down to the gates of the sea,
> Out of the gates of the west,

> Journeys the whispering river
> Before the place of his rest.

This is an elegy to someone who lived a simple life and enjoyed nature. The rhythm of this poem is most controlled, and for once Carman seems aware of the affinity between the sound and meaning of the words he is using. The words are general, the rhythm easy; there is no attempt to immerse the statement in archaic words or Arcadian references. It is an easy landscape the dead one has left behind, but his resting place is full of the things he loved. The picture from the graveyard is clear; the emotion is never maudlin:

> Then twilight falls with the touch
> Of a hand that soothes and stills,
> And a swamp-robin sings into light
> The lone white star of the hills.
>
> . . . .
>
> But there in the heart of the hills
> My beautiful weary one
> Sleeps where he laid him down;
> And the large sweet night is begun.

Perhaps this last line is precious, but it does control the poem and conclude the impression in a clear and masterful way.

The graveyard at Fredericton, on a hill overlooking the river—the one Carman liked and where he is buried—is the setting for the landscape picture presented in "The Grave-Tree." The first stanza gives Carman's wish, that was only honored by the University of New Brunswick twenty-five years after his death:

> Let me have a scarlet maple
> For the grave-tree at my head,
> With the quiet sun behind it,
> In the years when I am dead.

He follows the landscape as it would change through the year and through the day:

> Let me have the Silent Valley
> And the hill that fronts the east,

So that I can watch the morning
Redden and the stars released.

He looks upon the maple tree as a kind of haven at his last resting
place, one that will be his "leafy cabin"; as autumn comes, "Leaf
by leaf it will befriend me / As with comrades going home." The
tree will turn scarlet, deeper scarlet, in the autumn "when the
other world is near," and he hopes that it will show his love for
nature and his awareness of a mystical presence in it. The emotion
is ordinary, the image unclouded; to some it is trite. To Carman it
was an expression of a strong emotion; his desire for a scarlet
maple tree at his grave was very real to him; he could use the
poem to express this to his friends, who would not, perhaps, appreciate this departure from the Bohemian temperament:

> Then fear not, my friends, to leave me
> In the boding autumn vast;
> There are many things to think of
> When the roving days are past.
>
> Leave me by the scarlet maple,
> When the journeying shadows fail,
> Waiting till the Scarlet Hunter
> Pass upon the endless trail.

This was 1898 and Carman was thirty-seven; it was two years
before *Last Songs of Vagabondia* would come out; but they, too,
were marked with this pensive averageness.

The *Pipes of Pan* series shows Carman's whole imaginative vision; it is limited, however, because it is bound by his interest in
the mystical. Where Keats could use the mystical to produce
greater poetry, Carman was only able to let it curtail his imagination. He was forty when he started to produce this series, and it is
natural that at this age he was able to see the limitations of his
earlier work; he could see that it had too much variety to be
wholly successful, that he had been unable to integrate his poetic
directions into something concrete and whole. His themes had
been various; his best work had been sporadic. He could now see
that he must look at his work with a more careful eye; he must
aim for forms that were more exact and strong. He knew, also,

that he must have a framework to express his philosophy. Carman now was able to view his position as a poet, and his work itself, with a more comprehensive eye. His interest was no longer only in one poem, but in a group of poems. He wanted to create a full collection; this was his purpose in the five volumes of the *Pipes of Pan* series.

He was aiming for a dual achievement; he wanted to satisfy his essentially lyrical bent at which he knew he succeeded, yet he also aimed for an epic quality. He satisfies, at times, the lyrical intensity, but never catches the extensive epic character that he wanted. His purpose was to show that through many subjects, and with many forms, he could reveal his fundamental concept that there is present in the world a potential for harmony and it is man's purpose to discover and maintain this harmony. This potential is material, spiritual, and mystical, and is present in all things. It has been present in all aspects of life, from the earliest times to the present. It was present in pagan and ancient times, and is present in Christian and modern times. It is part of myth and legend, of man's thinking and desire. Everything has this cosmic core.

The *Pipes of Pan* was written to exalt this potential harmony, to illustrate it when the potential had been used and attained. Its purpose was to show those moments of unity between man and nature, both spiritually and materially, and to contrast them to the times when the unity was not achieved. It is basically a transcendental vision, and a difficult message to put across, let alone illustrate and define. Carman rarely succeeds with it; for the most part the poems have an abstraction that is monotonous; taken as Carman intended them, as groups, they are dull. Only individually, and then rarely, do they forge away from the diffuseness put upon them by Carman's overall scheme and purpose. The diffuseness, the abstractness, comes about as a result of the lack of direction given to the poems as a whole group, or in the separate five sections. There is little distinctive character to the worlds and things that Carman examines here; he gets lost showing the diversity of things meant to illustrate his theme. And so the looseness remains in his work; any semblance of tightness disappears after the first book in the series; he had not learned his lesson from the earlier works as well as he thought he had. Again, he was carried away by his own words, his own control of images and rhythms. He never did learn the lesson.

And so, instead of a series of connected poems, there is again a miscellaneous representation of his work in the series. He does start well, however, in the first book, *From the Book of Myths*, when he quite cleverly adapts the Pan myth as a symbol for the obscure relationship in man and nature of Earth and Spirit. He takes Pan, brings him up to date, and initially seems to equate him with what he calls an "overlord," something that is the integration of everything in body, spirit, and action on earth. He makes a catalogue of this "overlord" where he, the poet, will be:

> I who am dust and air
> Blown through the halls of death,
> Like a pale ghost of prayer,—
> I am thy breath.

Carman is "the word," "ending no song," and this role serves him throughout the whole series as he seeks to illustrate the power in life, the intangible he sees about him in his own age, and in the time before him. And Pan also becomes many things, as he says in the title poem, "The Pipes of Pan":

> Slowly hill and stream and wood
> Merged and melted, for my mood,
> With the colour of the sun
> In the pipe I played upon.

As a thrush, always "far solitary" or "hermit," Carman will examine the world and its many dimensions.

His focus in the first book of the series is to remove any ancient reminder of Pan, and to bring the idea of him into the reality of present day. He does this modernizing in many ways. Throughout the poems, he distributes Pan into modern images in which all the classical and Grecian associations disappear, though he does retrace the beginning of the myth with the pursuit of Syrinx and the invention of the pipe of the shepherd. Syrinx is a modern late nineteenth-century girl and Pan is alive with modern vigor. The lines, however, emphasize most strongly the desire for a contemporaneous quality; the couplet form is easy, the images reflect Carman's time. He seems to be deliberately swinging away from the use of classical imagery; all he wants is the controlling image and he demands that his readers see the influence and meaning of Pan in modern terms. It would have been easier, and more indicative of his classical background, to leave Pan in a classical setting; but Carman's intentions were to use the legend only to communicate a philosophy that has meaning in light of his own time, though it covers all time. The story of Pan is one of the few that Carman took and added to and reinterpreted for his own use; frequently he would take an idea and, more often than not, accept it as it was given to him or as he envisioned it; he rarely got to the core of it and never synthesized it into an original concept. Since Carman's time, the story has been used, but his approach to it is new and often quite vigorous. For Carman, Pan is identified with melancholy, the melancholy that accompanies growth as all mankind waits for a moment of epiphany or redemption; Pan signifies for him the Wordsworthian sense of the "still sad music of humanity." This is contrasted to the trend of most moderns who see Pan as a symbol of joy and fulfilment. Carman takes the aspect of fulfilment and brings to it the aspect of growth and pursues another dimension of it.

Carman could not take any limitation; he had to extend any idea beyond its meaning; this desire and need for extension was perhaps his greatest failure as a poet. It weakens this series, and it also brings about the lack of strength in much of his poetry both in form and theme. So he extravagantly expands the Pan myth because of his need for a variety of poetic illustration. Pan has too many meanings for Carman; he knows too many secrets; philosophically, Carman in a sense destroys the meaning of the myth by giving it too many interpretations. He uses the myth for an allegory to present his own poetic aspirations in "A Young Pan's Prayer" and identifies himself in numerous instances too closely to the story of Pan. Personalism is always ascendant in Carman; he continually is the focus of his own world and though he may at times try to point his attention to something greater—as he initially does in this series—he always returns to himself. Personalism is all right if moderate, but with Carman it is always extreme. He records his own experience almost as an autobiography, or he records experiences that he feels he should have, and often they bear minor references to things universal. There is a great deal of the universal in his poetry, through tradition and through the use of frameworks that are well known, as with Pan or Sappho. But the poetry becomes too personal and seems to shun an awareness of mass universals. His personalism becomes false and local and is embarrassingly revealing, yet it often conceals the man behind the poetry. Too often he is what he thinks others want him to be, not what he really is.

So the Pan legend, as used by Carman, brings the poet in to the poetry too strongly and becomes formless. The vague diffuseness destroys the potential that the myth has for modern readers. Carman does not have that rare combination of thinking and aesthetics to take the poetic atmosphere inherent in Pan and enlarge it into a meaningful interpretation of life. It is obvious from the first volume of the series that Carman was aware of this lack of integration with the myth, so that when he moves away from the myth completely his lyrical vigor returns. The subjects, eventually, have no connection with his reading of the Pan myth except that all life is part of Pan. The volume presents only occasional glimpses of Carman's better qualities, as when he brings notes of elegy to stories of Phaedra or Daphne. The volume becomes fragmentary and serves as a prophecy of the fragmentary quality that exists in the rest of the series.

The scheme was too vast for Carman, and the five volumes belie the title given to them. Most poets would have changed the title and admitted the mistake but not Carman; he obviously convinced himself that all was right with it. He felt the comprehensive quality of his reading of Pan could apply to anything, and consequently he threw anything in. Gone is any artistic unity, any logical development. The variety in tone and treatment of the volumes gives no continuity to the group. Rarely does his lyrical facility give any interior unity within the separate volumes. The whole series is fitful, and often merely obscure.

The second volume in the series, *From the Green Book of Bards,* 1903, takes Carman into the subject he likes to write about the most, spring songs and lyrics of nature. The volume has nothing to do with bards, except in the title poem which has a formlessness rarely equalled, full of every poetic cliché and archaism, and here again the ego emerges:

> One page, entitled Grand Pré,
> Has the idyllic air
> That Bion must have envied:
> I set a foot-note there.

But if Carman were the center of his universe, it was spring that held the cosmic position as a controlling factor over life. He saw it as the beginning of things, the time of freshness and newness. There is nothing original in this idea, but at times there is freshness in the expression. It was a magical time of year:

> Soon the hazy purple distance,
> Where the cabined heart takes wing,
> Eager for the old migration
> In the magic of the spring.
>   ("April Weather")

He catalogues the spring for the reader; he extols its beauty. Its mystical significance is associated again with Carman's ego; he was born in April; the month had larger significance. But as in "Spring Song," he was over-enthusiastic and shows lapses of taste. In "Spring Magic" he can be tritely poetic:

> I fade in silver music,
> Whose fine unnumbered notes
> The frogs and rainy fifers
> Blow from their reedy throats.

The whole volume is a calling from nature to all creatures, to all inanimate and animate things, to rise and join in celebration for beginnings. He gives the wind a strong role here; it becomes the significant symbol for life beginning again. In "The Word in the Beginning" Carman delineates the relationship of all nature to the wind within the human cycle of existence. At times his introduction of the wind symbol is extremely skilful:

> This is the sound of the Word
> From the waters of sleep,
> The rain-soft voice that was heard
> On the face of the deep,
> When the fog was drawn back like a veil, and
>   the sentinel tides
> Were given their thresholds to keep.[19]

The winds speak; the south wind says "Come forth," and the west wind says "Go far"; primarily he is working on the objective-transcendent levels of symbolic association. Through a sensitive description of physical reality, Carman suggests scriptural references and transcendent power. Spring is the time when things "gather for light," when the wind cannot be grasped as a physical object but is present in all things. The growth cycle of nature is suggested by nature's relationship with the wind and the spirit of things. But as spring is the time of beginning, it also has in it the suggestion of the end of things. The nature cycle is also destructive; the seeds of autumn are present in the beginnings of spring. So there is a melancholy associated with the inevitability of the life which spring brings.

He ends the volume by bringing in other seasons for contrast to spring, to reiterate the feeling of abundance which he associates with the "first season." He sees and feels the relationship among the seasons, when in the winter he can "harken for the winds of spring." Yet the spring songs have a sameness about them, as though the poet were seeking a new method of expression and not finding it; consequently, monotony persists in this volume. He paints, however, a familiar landscape, using traditional forms to express his feeling; he seems to be searching in his past for something to hold on to. It is not the New Canaan landscape he describes, but the one of New Brunswick that he sees—though actually there is a similarity between the two. From now on Carman would continue to reach back for memories and concepts which had meaning for him. He had stopped growing, both as a man and as a poet. Yet there is no desperation in his looking to the past; he does not clutch at it with weakening fingers, nor does he regret the necessity to do so. He does not philosophize about his need for finding something in the past. His life had become a routine; he had taken an easy road that was to culminate in his

friendship with Mary Perry King. He had reached the age of reflection, not of reflection on the present, but of deliberate turning
to the past. So he could end this volume of verse with references
to his mother, the strongest and most meaningful influence on his
life, in "After School."

> When all my lessons have been learned,
> And the last year at school is done,
> I shall put up my books and games;
> "Good-by, my fellows, every one!"
>
> The dusty road will not seem long,
> Nor twilight lonely, nor forlorn
> The everlasting whippoorwills
> That lead me back where I was born.
>
> And there beside the open door,
> In a large country dim and cool,
> Her waiting smile shall hear at last,
> "Mother, I am come home from school."

The lesson learned was that his own country, his own traditions,
his own ego, were most meaningful to him. Any chances for
breaking out of the mold were now gone. He could now only
reiterate the concepts that he had received in the past. From now
on the haunting flavor would grow; the symbolism would stay
the same; economy in phrase, theme, and image, would be lost.
Yet none of these poems is entirely superfluous; there is always
something in a poem which redeems it, as there is always something which shows his weakness at integrating his expression.

Songs of the Sea-Children, volume three in the *Pipes of Pan*
series, brings Carman back to his past, and does in a sense bring
him an opportunity to extend one of his better directions: the love
lyric. Before, the love poems were fused with pictures of nature,
and there was no eroticism to speak of. But in this volume of
poetry, he does become erotic, and does so because his concept of
love can be directly related to the scheme that he has for the
whole series. Love is associated with nature, to be sure, but as a
physical urge which is part of the scheme of things, so that he can
produce such lines as:

Thou art the fair seed vessel
Waiting all day for me,
Who ache with the golden pollen
The night will spill for thee.

("XXXIV")

I loved you when the auroral fire,
Like the world's veriest desire,
Burned up, and as it touched the sea,
You laid your limbs to mine.

("LIX")

It may seem that this is only a fanciful man playing with the idea of love.[20] He may be fooling, and the emotion often may be disguised by what he thinks his readers want, but undoubtedly the emotion expressed in the majority of these poems is not lukewarm. At times it almost has some pure fire:

Thy mouth is a snow apple,
Thy tongue a rosy melon core,
Thy breasts are citrons odorous of the East,
I know that nursery tale of Eden now,
Where God prepared the feast
Beneath the bow,
I ask no more.

("XL")

Though the green-grocer images are bad, the emotion is strong; no longer is there a veil as in the melancholic poems in *Low Tide on Grand Pré*. Carman obviously is delighting in what he has to say. Admittedly, the motions are the same, the monotony is present in the whole volume—mainly because there are too many poems—but he does show an individuality that is refreshing, and even at times quite stimulating.

In the previous love poems, in *Low Tide on Grand Pré* and in other books, there is the touch of melancholy about a love that is over, that is past. Formerly, the love relationship brought the poet pain, and separated him from the world. This awareness of himself as something separate, the awareness of his own short life-span, his helplessness before the forces of nature, makes Carman dwell on a kind of disunited existence. For a while he can unite himself with his world by talking about nature, by showing the affinity of his grief about a lost love with the tide, or the cycle of nature. But Carman has learned, in this volume, an invaluable lesson; his love poems concern a relationship that is going on in the present, that can defeat nature at her most depressing:

> Love, lift your longing face up through the rain!
> In the white drench of it over the hills,
> Blurring remembrance and quieting pain,
> Stretch the strong hands of the sea.
>
> Love, lift your longing face up through the rain!
> In the bleak rote of it through the far hills.
> Rhythmed to joy and untarnished of pain,
> Calls the great heart of the sea.
>
> ("XXXII")

Here is a love that implies care and attention, a love that is strong and meaningful, in the *now*.

It is easy to dismiss these lyrics, as critics have done, by saying that they are merely "lyrical sighs," limited in length. It appears, however, that Carman here was working within a framework that he could control. He had shown that he could not work with the long poem, that a poem with many stanzas becomes monotonous and repetitious. But here he gives the poems control by saying just one or two things in short stanzas; the form is simple, the rhyme and rhythm uncluttered. He takes love as the central experience of the "sea children," who see their relationship in terms of the world around the sea and its natural landscape. The love expressed does not stand still; it does not become fatuous and weak because it has a sameness about it. It is not love in the absence of conflict; they live in a world of storm and struggle, and because of this comparison their own love gains a greater meaning for them. And so the outer conflict leads to a deeper level of inner reality:

> I loved you when you stood tiptoe
> To say farewell, and let me go

Into the night from your laced arms,
And laid your mouth to mine.

And I shall love you on that day
The wind comes over the sea to say
Your golden name upon men's mouths,
And mix your dust with mine.

("LIX")

These poems are romantic; they often express the most repulsive overplay of emotion. Yet they are interesting in themselves as love poems, and more important, they do not reveal the strong narcissism that is present in many of Carman's other poems. Admittedly, the "I" is used frequently, but the concern seems to be with the duality of the relationship, with the two people involved. Carman seems, at long last, to have grown up. And with this maturity comes a keener vision. The images are less trite: "She had the tender bearing/ Of daffodils in spring"; "a moon white moth against the moon"; "Once more the woods grow crimson,/ Once more the year burns down." The images are less contrived; they assume a spontaneity rarely found in the rest of his work. He seems to have achieved, in this volume at least, the ability to give his poems a polished yet impromptu quality. Before, the style and the form were conspicuous. In this volume they are lost in the beauty of the whole poem. He does, unfortunately, bring his ego back with the last poem, but the beauty of the image softens that fault; he feels that the poems will be:

Teasing the sullen years
Out of monotony,
As reedbirds pour their rapture
By the unwintered sea.

("Aftersong")

In the fourth volume in this series, Carman deliberately returns to the Canadian landscape, but he had been doing so for some time; his landscape is always touched with New Brunswick shapes and colors. *Songs From a Northern Garden* is Carman's attempt at deliberately introducing Pan into the Canadian scene, extending his idea that Pan is everywhere. The volume becomes overwrought by its deliberateness, however, and the fantasy is extended too far. He tries, too, for heavy rhythms that destroy the theme the poem is trying to produce:

> So I get my myth and legend of a breaker-down
>   of bars,
> Putting gateways in the mountains with their
>   thousand-year-old scars,
> That the daring and the dauntless might steer
>   Outward by the stars.
>   ("In A Grand Pré Garden")

He could not produce the simple rhythms of the *Sea Children* for an extended time, and it is easy to see why he changed; he did not want to be accused of lack of variety again. Housman added to his reputation by doing so, but Carman was not a Housman. Rarely does he capture in this volume the essence of "Sea Children." At times, however, the images have the freshness of the previous work:

> There are sunflowers too in my garden on top of the hill,
> Where now in early September the sun has his will,—
> The slow autumn sun that goes leisurely, taking his fill
> Of life in the orchards and fir woods so moveless and still:
>   ("Above the Gaspereau")

The last line is bad, but the first one has a poignant beauty.

But it is with this volume that familiarity sets in with the reader of Carman. From now on there would always be echoes of an earlier Carman; with *Songs of the Sea Children* the bolt had been shot. Eventually his poetry becomes predictable, as it is in *Songs From a Northern Garden.* There is a thrush for comparison to the poet, a piping frog, scarlet maple trees, sea-birds at the setting of the sun. The tone is one of nostalgia, of looking back at another time which even then was not so happy. He implies that "It will be, perhaps, pleasant to remember even these things." The spirit will survive despite conflicts with nature if man learns to love, to value friendship. Death will be a beginning; goodbye means hello to something new. Man can learn from nature; she is a teacher, minister, nurse, friend. When nature is silent there is communion with something beyond. This something is at times a transcendental being and other times the Christian God. When there is a didactic note in the poetry, the tone is that of Browning, the form that of the monologue. Every poem has some good lines, and some of the verses can be removed without destroying the poem in any way. There is a tendency toward redundancy and monotony, although the occasional image and line has a fine beauty. There is rarely ever any animation. The naïveté continues, becomes more pronounced, and his occasional lyrical burst becomes uncertain.

Piety overtakes Carman in *Songs From a Northern Garden*. He sermonizes in some poems that are too long—"Christmas Eve at St. Kavin's" is sixty stanzas in length—and his message is unoriginal. He cannot extend the biblical message of love beyond its ordinary limits, not even to Auden's "we must love one another or die." It is consistent that he attain this reverence when he is dealing with church legends concerning French Canada, but often his religion becomes too obvious. It is useful when he starts a poem for introduction and setting, and to acknowledge the titles of the poems—"The Ballad of Father Hudson," "The Word at St. Kavin's," "St. Bartholomew's On the Hill"—but then he seems to come up short and remember that he is writing a volume of verse belonging to a series which has Pan as the central figure. The lack of unity between the two themes weakens both to the degree that neither is very successful. In "Christmas Eve at St. Kavin's" he is discussing the sermon given by a young priest to celebrate the birth of Christ, for "The House of Many Mansions holds us all"; this religious metaphor becomes more than earthly, however, when Carman takes the message of love and transforms it into the "new word/ The Syrian twilight heard":

> Believe the truth of love,
> Enact the beauty of love,
> Praise and adore the goodliness of love.
> For we are wise by love,
> And strong and fair through love,
> No less sainted and inspired with love.

This tone is strengthened again in the last volume of the series, *From the Book of Valentines*. He returns to the cosmic vision which began the series in the first place; but he is compromising his position as a poet. He did not dare to stop the series that had begun because he was working with ideas that could only be repeated and not extended; at least, Carman could only repeat them. He compromises himself, too, when he uses recurrent themes and repeated images. No doubt, if the thought is not too deep, there cannot be too much variety in scope as to form and statement. But frequently the descriptions of landscape could be interchanged at will throughout the whole five volumes of the series. Carman seems to use indifferently the principle of selection, which is, after all, the greatest tool of the poet and the one which makes him great. The reader would not mind perusing the repeated ramblings of a poet as long as they reached out into new worlds; Carman's repetition does not have this quality, nor is it for emphasis. The peculiar feeling is that he was not interested any more. It is as though he were caught in a web of his own making, struggled for a while to release himself, and failing, held on to what remained with diffidence. So the repetition continues in the last volume; only once was he able to rouse himself and that was only to recall the qualities of *Songs of the Sea Children* in *Sappho*.

Canada again serves as the landscape in *From the Book of Valentines*. It is a land where "there lived a sturdy folk by the borders of the sea." Carman tries in this poem to make the landscape picture-postcard Scandinavian: "The snow tipped mountains behind them guarding the East and the North." There is the mystery of other volumes; "This window has been sealed up so/ A fortnight now." He asserts:

> Spring's return,
> When daffodils and jonquils burn
> Under the azure April day
> Is not more lovely nor more gay.

It is another April, another Spring; the sky is azure, the daffodils and jonquils are in bloom. The tone of melancholy is heard in "To One in Despair" and "At the Great Release"; he persists with the occasional classical allusion to carry on the Pan theme. He continues with the double adjectives ("great gusty," "passionate eternal") and the heavy language ("mordant unassuaged"). The "first tawny thrush" reappears, with "his reed pipe, eerie calm and golden." The references to death are strong in this volume, too. In "The Least of Love," "A Man's Last Word," and "An Angel in Plaster," the tone is one of a writer saying farewell. And in many ways, this last volume of the series is a farewell; the rest of the poetry only rarely recapitulates the last stanza of the volume:

> Yet thou must tarry here, thou darling one,
> To smile and bring
> Thoughts of the world's far youth, a fadeless sun
> And a perpetual spring.

For some readers, the tarrying is too long.

In his next major work of verse, the undertaking of a restoration of the lyrics of Sappho, Bliss Carman set himself a difficult task. Since the seventh century B.C., when the Lesbian culture reflected in her poems ceased to exist, Sappho has been alternately praised and damned. The Greeks considered her the greatest of the lyric poets. For Plato, Sappho was the tenth muse. Though the Romans had condemned her and her poetry—and especially her life—the scholars of Carman's time took a new interest in her life and poetry. Their interest was in the ambiguity of Sappho's character; though the age, the "dark age of Greece," was condemned, for the perversions of its women, nothing of this can be seen in the fragments left of Sappho.

The only extant literature from Sappho's Lesbos are her own poems and the lyrics of Alcaeus; Carman sought, in reconstructing the poems of Sappho, an evaluation of a woman whose nature had been the subject of debate for centuries and who lived in a culture whose values were alien to his own. The method would be, as given by Roberts in his introduction to the Sappho lyrics,

To imagine each lost lyric as discovered and then to translate it; for the indefinable flavour of the translation is maintained throughout, though accompanied by the fluidity and freedom of purely original work.[21]

The "indefinable flavour of translation" is responsible for the stiffness—and in some cases, the coldness—of many of the poems in the volume, and of poems elsewhere.

[74]

The original fragments are translated closely, but the warmth and tenderness of the model is often lost. In Lyric LXIII, Carman writes:

> A beautiful child is mine,
> Formed like a golden flower,
> Cleis the loved one.
> And above her I value
> Not all the Lydian land,
> Nor lovely Hellas.

Sappho was writing of her daughter. To her Cleis was not "the loved one" but "dear Cleis"; Sappho does not "value" her; she says that she loves Cleis better than all the wealth of Lydia, or the beauty of Hellas.

Again, in Lyric VI, Carman fails to capture the fire and intensity of the original. In the Lesbian fragment, a self-critical, observant nature is revealed; in the opening line the jealous nature of her character appears. In Carman there is none of this; he weakens the translation seriously; gone is the fire. His added verses are imaginatively reconstructed, but he has failed to capture the essence of Sappho; it is difficult to imagine a woman of concrete and refined expression picturing herself as an "adventurous sailor." The "lure of the summer and the sea's secret" are Carman's usual nature symbols of life and death, but Sappho, as far as we know, never used nature in this symbolic fashion.

Carman's interpretation of Sappho is one-sided. In Lyric V, a close translation of Fragment 1, he fails to bring out the self-mocking humor of Sappho. Carman evokes Aphrodite, the "willful empress," "praying" her to come with her, "fleet sparrows beating the mid air/ Over the dark earth." Suddenly, the goddess is near; smiling, she asks "—why I had called . . .—" "What fair thing wouldst thou lure now to love thee?" Carman's "willful empress" has none of the suggestiveness of Sappho's "wile weaving Aphrodite." His vision of the questions put by the goddess is far more gracious than Sappho's. Her goddess asks, "What ails you *now?* Whom must I persuade to love you *now?*" Sappho's goddess smiles too, but she is amused, and just a little impatient. In Sappho, not only the goddess, but the sparrows—sparrow-flesh was eaten as an aphrodisiac—are near. Sappho, though suffering the pain and anguish of love, laughs at her own vanity and fickleness.

Lyric LIII does not represent restoration, but demonstrates Carman's ability to select two fragments, weld them together, and use them to express his own idea of love:

> Art thou the top-most apple
> The gatherers could not reach,
> Reddening on the bough?
>   Shall not I take thee?
>
> Art thou a hyacinth blossom
> The shepherds upon the hills
> Have trodden into the ground?
>   Shall not I lift thee?
>
> Free is the young god Eros,
> Paying no tribute to power,
> Seeing no evil in beauty,
>   Full of compassion.
>
> Once having found the beloved,
> However sorry or woeful,
> However scornful of loving,
>   Little it matters.

James Cappon[22] suggests that Carman was inspired to put these two fragments together with their essentially different pathos and change the contemplative sympathy of Sappho into an egotistical interest on behalf of the lover. The two fragments, which are stanzas one and two, are Sappho, 150, 151. He has interpreted them correctly, and has added his own concept of meaning to them.

Most of the "Sappho lyrics" written by Carman are not translations, or even restorations, but are "free inventions," sometimes inspired by a line of Sappho, sometimes not. They tend toward vague generalization; detail is forgotten; journeys are taken but to nowhere, lovers are together but for no reason. Sappho was never vague. But though some of the group should never have been included in such a collection, others are among the best of all

Carman's poetry. In LIV, an expression of the poet's passion for life and hatred of death, the maritime landscape which Carman knew is blended with sensuous metaphors Sapphic in their intensity. A similar technique is used in XXIII, which was inspired by Fragment 48: "I loved you Atthis, long ago, when all my own girlhood was still all flowers, and you—you seemed to me a small ungainly child." For Carman it is:

> I loved thee, Atthis, in the long ago,
> When the great oleanders were in flower
> In the broad herded meadows full of sun.

Landscape is important to both of these poets, not in itself, but for the mood and atmosphere which it may evoke. It is through their use of landscape that a fundamental difference in the mood of the two sets of poems is revealed. Sappho presents a radiant "lightsome" world, shining with gold, and sunlight, and silver. Her gold is the "child of Zeus," the light with which the sun-god "illumines the earth with his down-shed flame outspread," and her silver, the light of the moon: "around the fair moon the bright beauty of the stars is lost when her silver light illumines the world at its fullest." Hers is a world vivid with purple robes, and saffron smocks, a world touched with hyacinthine blue, and the black richness of the earth. Aphrodite is golden, the Graces are rose-ankled, and the breasts of women are violet sweet. It is a world where the whirring of sparrows may be heard, and the rustling of breezes; where the sweet-toned flute mingles with the sound of the rattle, and a sweet shrill song purrs from beneath the wings of a cricket.[23]

In comparison, Carman's world is soft and muted. Autumn colors the earth and sunlight sleeps in the vineyard; the olive grove is grey and the birds are brown; shadows trail and the sun is silver. But though it lacks the radiance of Sappho's landscape, Carman's has a tender beauty of its own. He knows of "broad herded meadows full of sun" at a time when "the soft grass heads were all wet with dew and purple misted in the fading light"; where a traveler "might emerge from the deep green seclusion of the hills, and on a sudden, turning a great rock,/ Covered with grondage, dark with dripping water/ Behold the seaboard full of surf and sound,/ With all the space and glory of the world/ Above the burnished silver of the sea." The landscape of Carman's world differs from that of Sappho's, and its sounds are different, too. He hears the sounds of the sea. "Plunging in thunderous onset to the shore . . . ," the sea with its "pealing gulls," and on land he hears the "chattering oak leaves" and a "tinkling Eastern wind-bell."

Another fundamental difference between the two poets lies in their use of symbolism. To Carman *nature* is a symbol, a symbol of the cycle of life. He relates emotion to the appropriate season. Sappho is aware of the cycle of nature, too, but to her, in the Adonis lyrics, the gods are real beings and the death of Adonis represents the dying of the year with little symbolic overtone. Aphrodite was a real and powerful goddess, who in her own way stood for absolute values, for a kind of magic which gives to life and to men a desire that almost drives them mad. This kind of epiphany to Sappho was a poetic convention used to add vividness to her work. She believed that gods came down to earth and interfered in the lives of men; it was more than a simple poetic and epic convention; it proved her faith.

To Carman, this is a concept impossible to reflect in his poetry because of his transcendental view of "God within man." He uses the ancient gods as symbols. Pan is a symbol of goodness inherent in Nature, the "Protector of hers in the meadows/ Helper of men at their toiling." He is also the maker of "magic music." Carman is not always too careful in his concept of the ancient deities. Sappho mentions Hermes only in his traditional role of messenger of the gods and wine-bearer for them. Carman makes him "often the giver of secret learning to mortals." There is a curious lapse in XCI where Carman uses the name "Saturn." Since the name of Saturn's Greek counterpart, Kronos, is metrically equivalent to "Saturn," Carman must have considered one name more euphonious than the other.

Sappho is a true lyricist. Her purpose in writing was to express in perfectly chosen words what she felt in moments of concentrated insight and strained excitement. There is, as in most of Carman's poetry, the element of the didactic. He often reflects Sappho's idea that death is an evil or else the gods themselves would die. But he is naturally more concerned with his own viewpoint; not for him the practical thoughts of Sappho, such as the view that a blending of wealth and worth is the top of fortune. Instead he uses ideas more easily adapted to his own concepts, as when he reflects Sappho's weariness of exile in Lyric XXXIX:

> The heart of man must seek and wander,
> Ask and question and discover knowledge;
> Yet above all goodly things is wisdom,
> And love greater than understanding.

Another example is found in LVIII:

> The gods themselves and the almightier fates
> Cannot avail to harm
>
> . . . .
>
> The radiant unshaken mind of him
> Who at his being's centre will abide,
> Secure from doubt and fear.

There is no mention of Fate in Sappho; undoubtedly she shared the Greek concept of μοτρα as an inflexible power beyond the control of even the mightiest of the gods. Carman's lyric results from his view that God and freedom lie within man's "self."

Carman makes frequent use of the short, light Adonic line and of the swift-moving variant of the Glyconic, but he did not attempt the formal imitation of Sappho's meter; he had probably seen the disaster that Tennyson's attempts to reproduce the Alcaic meter had wrought.

It is in theme that Sappho and Carman come closest together, but this does not bring too much proximity. Sappho sought to reveal loves and hatreds, the ephemeral pleasures and pains of her time, the passion for favorites. If Carman's motive for his Sappho was indeed to restore the poetry of the ancient Lesbian, he has been only partially successful. He reveals only one facet of her character, using only those fragments which reflect his own search for beauty. He seizes upon the mystery surrounding Sappho's relationships with men and women to interpret Sappho according to his whim at the moment of composition. He gives no clear, consistent picture of Sappho. Many of his lyrics are just more of his "spring songs," or reflections of his own experience. But in a few lyrics, such as XXIII, he has given a unique and successful blending of what is best in Carman and best in Sappho. The collection proves his statement in *The Friendship of Art:*

We must remember that all art, like life itself, is a compromise—a compromise between what we would and what we can.[24]

For a while (1905–1909) Carman, influenced by Mary Perry King, wrote prose essays[25] to reveal his philosophy. He returned to poetry in 1909 with *The Rough Rider and Other Poems,* following with *Echoes From Vagabondia* in 1912 and *April Airs* in 1916. For the most part these volumes are reflections of his earlier work, particularly of those themes in his poetry which Mary Perry King found most attractive. He was fifty years old in 1911; from a popular and productive poet one would expect evidence of a strengthened style. Carman, however, appears to have stayed very much the same. The lyrical quality is the same, the images similar; only in the tone is there any change, and that is minor. The mystical element is very much subdued. He has pursued this interest long enough, he seems to say, and has concluded that further pursuit will be valueless. He continues to return to physical reality, to the natural world around him. The transcendentalism, the pantheism, is almost gone; in its place comes a statement that is for the most part purely descriptive. Where formerly in the description of nature he would make reference to an oversoul, he is now content to allow metaphor to extend his thought. At times it is only personification:

> Time out of mind I have stood
> Fronting the frost and the sun,
> That the dream of the world might endure,
> And the goodly will be done.
>
> . . . .
>
> Lovers have leaned on me
> Under the summer moon,
> And mowers laughed in my shade
> In the harvest heat at noon.
>
> . . . .
>
> Ah, when will ye understand,
> Mortals who strive and plod,—

> Who rest on this old gray wall
> Lays a hand on the shoulder of God!

In this poem, "The Old Gray Wall," the presence of God in nature strikes the same chord of recognition in the reader as it does in "Vestigia," Carman's most popular and widely anthologized poem. This is the Carman that the Canadian reader remembers, mainly perhaps because the poem is in every school reader. The thought is simple, even sweet; the concept is trite, but compelling and obviously memorable:

> I took a day to search for God,
> And found Him not. But as I trod
> By rocky ledge, through woods untamed,
> Just where one scarlet lily flamed,
> I saw His footprint in the sod.

The poet discovers that "God dwelt within my heart." There is no attempt here to immerse the thought in philosophical questionings of the unknown to carry the idea along through emphasis until it is lost, as previously; he seems to have accepted that his thought is only pantheistic. In his maturity he can marvel simply over the wonder of God. He is content to present the spiritual experience, not examine it until it is without meaning.

The form becomes more simple, too. He goes back again to one of his earlier and stronger influences, the early Victorian lyric. Everything about the form is measured and simple; rarely does he improvise with the meter or the cadence of line. He uses, too, a contemplative blank verse that is regular, and only varies slightly from it. The unity of the poems is more singular; he seems to be better able to approximate tone with theme by using images that lift the poem along. Though the images are more or less pure Carman, and predictable, they produce a clearer outline for the poem. This is the work of a poet who is not concerned with what the public may want, who does not have to produce poetry because it is demanded of him. This is poetry produced in repose, by a man who may be pictured seated in a wicker chair, glasses in hand, a tartan rug tossed lightly over his lap:

> Over the dikes and the uplands
> Wander the great cloud shadows,
> Strange as the passing of sorrow,
> Beautiful, solemn, and slow.
>
> For, spreading her old enchantment
> Of tender ineffable wonder,
> Summer is there in the Northland!
> How should my heart not know?
>   ("A Remembrance")

The landscape is more clearly defined; the hazy hills have given
way to a cleaner horizon. The sentiment is less melancholic, less
susceptible to the moods of the pale-faced poet. In "A Mountain
Gateway," strength and vigor prevails, especially in the description itself:

> The road winds in from the broad river-lands,
> Luring the happy traveller turn by turn
> Up to the lofty mountains of the sky.
> And as he marches with uplifted face,
> Far overhead against the arching blue
> Gray ledges overhang from dizzy heights
> Scarred by a thousand winters and untamed.

He still uses spring as a predominant and unifying theme in his
verse, as in "Across the valley in the dusk / I hear the silver flute of
spring," but his use of it is less esoteric; it gains a simplicity with
maturity. He still aims to extend its meaning, but he confines himself to more acceptable metaphors. In "Resurgam" he writes, "Lo,
now comes the April pageant / And the Easter of the year."

For a time in these later poems Carman seems to flounder, looking for something to replace the mysticism he used to think was so
essential to his interpretation of life. He finds it, on one hand, by
re-echoing the earlier *Vagabondia* series in *Echoes From Vagabondia*, and on the other, by expressing in his poetry a more pronounced attitude of resignation to the world as it is. A tranquillity
that often marks old age is present in one of his later and best
poems: "The Wood Thrush." Here he is restating his previously
expressed ideas; he uses the thrush again, and he looks for mean-

ing in the spring. But there is nothing to mar the flow of the line, no borrowed phrase, no archaic expression. The words are simple and restrained; insincere affectation of the poet's role is not present here. Simplicity marks the picture as it marks the atmosphere of the poem:

> Hark, from the twilit wood beyond the road,
> Those leisurely enraptured cadences
> Borne on the dust deliberate and pure,
> As if the player in long ages past
> Knowing all grief had learned to put it by,
> In a calm melody where no fear is.
> That is our wood-thrush who each year returns
> To be the heart's interpreter of Spring.
> Minstrel of solitude and poet's lore,
> His is the music of unspoken things.
> Hark how the minor tenderness of time
> Old wistful longings and the storied years,
> Blend in untarnished gladness, melt and sing
> The unembittered rapture of the hour.

Carman continues to show his idealistic nature; he believes that the world is a great and wonderful place and could become greater through our careful scrutiny of the traditions of the past. Today, his transcendental philosophy is out-dated; the twentieth century lacks the optimism it requires. Yet Carman can, in these last poems, recognize that pain is part of existence; he was always able to do this even in the early poems. But now it is said with a greater strength, and not oversentimentalized by poetic tricks. In "Triumphalis" he writes:

> Soul, art thou sad again
> With the old sadness?
> Thou shalt be glad again
> With a new gladness,

He does have strong hope, but emphasizes it without provinciality:

> Thou shalt take heart again,
> No more despairing;

Play thy great part again,
Loving and caring.
Hark, how the gold refrain
Runs through the iron strain,
Splendidly daring!

Thou shalt grow strong again,
Confident, tender,—
Battle with wrong again,
Be truth's defender,—
Of the immortal train,
Born to attempt, attain,
Never surrender.

At times in his *Later Poems*, he turns away from the distinguished lyricism which brought him to the public eye, and attempts to relate himself more closely to what is going on in his own time. He tries to join the tide of those presenting the average life in a realistic and informal fashion. Lyric romanticism was dead; Carman knew that he could not raise it from the dead. So he does try to present a more concrete picture of things, avoiding the mystical and high-flown quality of his other work. This rarely comes off, however; he sounds too much like Browning in these poems, and the sonnets of the period are too fragmentary to be successful. The romanticism remains.

His only real departure from the romantic tradition lies in his prose, but even that is touched with the romantic philosophy. In prose essays he could steer away from the outward marks of romanticism; the prose, however, is highly repetitive of his poetry in thought; often it appears that he repeated ideas in his prose because he was afraid that the poetry did not quite tell it all. Urged on by Mary Perry King, he collected groups of essays into little volumes ("They will make nice gifts," she said), the most prominent being *The Kinship of Nature*, 1904, *The Friendship of Art*, 1904, and *The Poetry of Life*, 1905.

Poetry, however, should not need prose essays to strengthen it. After all, Carman had said all he wanted to say in his poetry, and there is no doubt of what he meant. There may be occasional lapses in clarity, but these are always removed, often by the very redundancy of the statement. Still, Carman felt that he must play

with the aesthetic essay, and play with it he did. He could handle
the essay in anything but an ingenious fashion, and he was able to
ramble, to make extravagant statements, and to achieve the variety that he aimed for in his poetry. In many ways the essays are
apologies for his poetry, as though he felt the poetry needed
defending.

First of all, the essays defend his position as a poet. His aim, he
tells the reader, is to create beauty. This, he feels, is best done by
bringing the natural world into focus around him. Consequently,
he turns to nature as his main source of imagery. He attempts to
defend his conservative literary background and his attitudes
about human behavior. He tries, too, to defend his mysticism, his
transcendentalism. Above all, his essays aim at explaining away,
with all sincerity, his tendency toward an optimistic view of life.
Nature rewards man; it brings him to reality:

> Go into the park or the woods any morning, and listen until you hear
> a single rainbird soloing plaintively. . . . That is the strain which
> pierces the heart and plays upon the soul. It finds us as we are, not as
> we seem. And unless we are wholly corrupted and sodden with civiliza-
> tion, it wakens glimmerings of the golden age within us. . . .[26]

Here the direct affinity between the prose and the poetry is seen;
he says repeatedly in his verse that spring and nature are the best
experiences of men, and he says it again in his prose. He becomes
over-enthusiastic, talking of "a thousand departed Aprils" asleep
in the "placid veins." It is too much. Such ecstasy is little merited
in poetry; it has no place in prose. Particularly it is out of place in
an age steeped in the tradition of the great Victorian prose
writers. What would Ruskin think of such things? He would be
appalled. And even Oscar Wilde would find it all too "golden."
This interest in lavish language points toward the greatest weakness in the prose pieces. The interest of the writer is too much in
the words he uses, not in the total effect, or for that matter, in the
reason for which he is bothering to tell it all in prose. Carman
does not seem to know why he is telling it, and for that reason, the
prose is forced. He seems to have learned that one of the first rules
of good writing is to pay attention to words, but has not gone
beyond the first rule. So the whole quality of the prose is misdi-

BLISS CARMAN

rected by his own ignorance of what he is doing, of what he
should be doing. Mary Perry King was no doubt urging him on,
and he was thinking about those carefree hours around the evening fire when he would read what he had written that day. Two
or three pages would be the limit of one day's work. So there
appears about the prose a constantly elevated pitch, and the pitch
is not sustained. It becomes too fragmentary; even the essay as a
form of expression demands more integration, more logic, more
control.

Nonetheless, sometimes the style is quite pleasant, and it does
have its occasional high points. While organization and syntax are
not among them, occasionally the descriptive words are chosen
with care: there are the "soft spring mornings" where "pealing
cadence thrills on the damp air." So, his ability to "pay attention
to words" emphasizes his strong points while it reveals his weak
ones.

These essays—in *The Kinship of Nature,* and some in *The
Friendship of Art*—are written in the style of Lamb, and they
ramble with a familiar grace. It is the critical essays—concerning
art and literature—which are sterile in concept, style, and content.
For him, truth, beauty and moral content are essential to all art;
he is absolute in his creed and allows little release from it. For
him, the artist must attain a "perfect personality," and though he
realizes that this is impossible, he says that always for the artist
"art, is a difficult matter" and is the "embodiment of perfection." [27]
How perfectly ridiculous! That Carman thought this kind of statement was worth saying is a wonder. Yet he said it. Hovering in the
background of these essays is the simpering "magic wonder" of
Mary Perry King; what a horror she must have been with her grey
gossamer dresses and solicitous manner. She talked constantly either of Carman or of her school of personal development. A mind
preoccupied with such a woman and with such foolish ideas could
not be very selective in its own productions. So the prose rambles;
it is erratic and full of secondary visions. He asks his readers not
to read Ibsen; he makes paradoxical statements about Carlyle
without reason or proof. He was not a sage yet, but he was certainly acting like one.

And it is Mary Perry King who created the sage, and Carman,
because he liked her, began to believe her. Only rarely did he go

against her wishes, as when he went on his Canadian tour in the twenties. But his egoism was returning, and she satisfied it for him. As a writer avowedly searching for harmony, he does not seem to find it in his own thinking. Instead, he compromises. With his lady friend standing over him, watching every word he wrote, catering to his every whim, it is no wonder that he produced what can be called "unadulterated drivel." There is one particular example of this kind of writing, in both style and content, but particularly in content, which shows how the prose lacks any conviction or integrity. For Carman, the artist who was insincere was "beyond the pale of human sympathy." [28] To be insincere was morally wrong. Admittedly "sincerity" is difficult to establish in view of the function of the artist. Carman often did not practice what he preached. He often took the ideas of others, often because he agreed with them, of course, but also because he knew that their ideas would be acceptable to a reading public. He contributed to the *Vagabondia* series because he felt the public would want that kind of poetry. His love poetry often raises doubts of sincere experience, let alone sincere emotion. His artistic appearance—the turquoise jewelry, the long hair—was very much a pose. Yet he was the one who felt sincerity was a very important aspect, the most important one for the poet. He contends that poetry should be "optimistically joyful," yet his most sincere poetry is sad and melancholic. Against this, in *The Poetry of Life* he says that a person should always smile, even "if it be insincere." One of the greatest questions raised by Carman's poetry—and his prose—is the one of sincerity. Often, it appears that it is all a mask; the man never shows through.

Though these paradoxes do exist in both his prose and poetry, the former, like the latter, does have the occasional flawless statement. It is very easy to read, though it does get dull after a while. For him, "fact is solidified fancy," a statement expertly stated, abundantly felt. He can freshly express feeling and thought in his verse. But it is a too casual manner, a sweetness that becomes heavy. The continued casualness turns sour. The full-bodied quality of his poetry merges with his final prose pieces and they become one and the same. There is, after all, no final difference between the two forms for Carman. He wrote his prose as a poet and could not distinguish between the two techniques of expression. Both are full of a strong spiritual—it is not emotional—quality. The transcendental philosophy is omnipresent in both. He does not have the astringency often possessed by women writers, nor does he have a strong masculine quality. His quality is sweet, poignant, fleeting. Peculiar inconsistencies mark the thought as they mark the style. There is the heavy luxuriance of the words, yet the lyrical suggestiveness is rarely equalled in Canadian letters. So much is suggested in Carman's lines. This is because he rarely, if ever, seems to know where he is going. For him, finally, the method is more important than the content, and so any concept of wholeness is lost. The vacillation between many things leads him to fragmentary comments about various parts of life. He could never find a direction. He can be biblical in tone, then colloquial; his attitude to his reader is at one time restrained, then familiar and personal. This leads to his best point: native simplicity. When he is able to tastefully fuse style and thought, he illustrates a native charm.

But simple it remains. There is rarely anything of depth in Carman. The world he inhabited both physically and in his imagination is the same world. He is unlike those poets—Keats for instance—who create worlds far removed from their own. Carman's imagination infrequently took him away from his own world—as in *Pan* or *Sappho*—but he was at his best when his two worlds fused. His imagination was not strong enough, his intellect not cultivated enough, to carry him into a metaphoric world of grand expression and great poetry. His country is New Brunswick and New England, and it is the world he inhabits both in his mind and in his body. But he is able to bring this world to the mind of his reader as very few before him were able to do. Whitman and Emerson gave a part of New England to the world, but not its ordinary reality; Whitman's private world could have been anywhere; Emerson was not the first transcendentalist. The actuality of the landscape is almost uncannily vivid in Carman. He does this with the simple phrase, noticing things in the landscape that any observer would see. Admittedly, he selects the things for his reader to see, but always they are the ordinary things, the points in the landscape which anyone would notice. He has filled this vision with misty people, with misty emotions, yet is able to capture the awakening that both the world and the people in it feel when winter is over and spring has come. It is because he does not fool with his imagination, does not let it create for him an unreality, that he is able to describe it so closely. For him, the landscape always "whispers," as in truth landscape always does.

CHAPTER 4

Influences

Everything in Carman's training and temperament tended to attach him to the older tradition in literature . . . even his style and methods of composition when they have the most individuality show respect for the standards of older literature.

—JAMES CAPPON [1]

THERE is a specific problem of influences in the poetry of Bliss Carman. His verse is so highly derivative that it is sometimes impossible to assess any particular influence. There are many echoes of previous poets in all of Carman's verse. A reader is soon reminded of a phrase, an adjective, or a thought encountered in the poems of major poets. Because of the many overtones, the direct influence is frequently lost. In trying to trace thought to a direct source, the reader becomes easily confused. These shades or echoes in Carman's poetry are often obvious because he created his poems with specific atmospheres in mind. Whether consciously or unconsciously created, the mood of a Carman poem is often much the same as that invented by other poets. In "Pulvis et Umbra" the mood resembles that of Edgar Allan Poe, yet there is nothing definite that substantiates this identification; without mystical haunted houses with bats, secret rooms, or ghost-like visions, the tone of this poem is nevertheless characteristically Poesque. This problem is encountered in many of Carman's poems. They have subtle connotations which are mainly Wordsworthian, Keatsian, or Emersonian (to name a few) in general atmosphere, but the direct source and effect of the influence is difficult to establish. Although the tone is often reminiscent of other poets, the freshness of Carman's images and the occasional passages of refined poetry hide the direct cause of the many principal influences on Carman's verse.

Most critics and biographers of Carman tend to divide his

poetry into three distinct phases; an early and strongly Romantic period, followed by one of excessive rationalism, which was in turn synthesized into his last phase, which included the best qualities of the first and second. This analysis seems accurate if the published works are followed chronologically. The first phase may be said to contain *Low Tide on Grand Pré* (1893) and the *Vagabondia* volumes (1894–96). The second period starts with *Behind the Arras* (1895) and ends with *The Green Book of the Bards* (1898). The later period includes the volumes of *Sappho* (1903) and the *Book of Myths* (1902). This distribution of phases, such as they are, seems more to say that there was little development in Carman's work, since the last period is a summation of the first two. This is true; there is no development or growth in Carman's poetry. It remained static throughout his entire career because of his tendency to follow the footpaths of others, to accept readily the traditions and statements of other people. A prime example of this—as has been seen—is in the *Vagabondia* poems; they point up the discrepancy between Carman's life and his works. He was too weak and dependent a personality to live and enjoy the rugged, rustic life. It seems better to say that Carman's work ranges through various patterns of creativity.

The dominant qualities of his poetry are present in each volume, and he never completely discards any aspect of his verse. Rarely are there germs of a later and different Carman in an early poem; ideas present in the beginning of his work are also present in the later poems. Carman's intention was to wait until he had a group of poems of the same tone, atmosphere, and style before he published them. Perhaps this plan was unwise, for the individual volumes tend to become staid and monotonous in effect. In a well selected collection of his poetry this monotony can be avoided for the most part, and the freshness of the various atmospheres retained. If at one time, a volume was published in a Romantic strain, the critic cannot assume that all the poetry written at that time was in the same Romantic one; nor, if the volumes written in a period of excessive rationalism are studied, can it be presupposed that the poetry of that period was all equally rational in tone.

These periods or phases mentioned by Carman's critics, are

surely, and more reasonably so, patterns of style and thought. Toward the end of his life these distinct patterns came close together but they did not culminate into one well-wrought poem, or one as well integrated as "Low Tide on Grand Pré," the title piece of his first volume published in 1893 and privately printed in much the same form in 1887. Carman never learned to save the best and leave behind the poorest, to create a new poetic unity in his later poetry.[2] All the primary elements of Carman's poetry were with him at the beginning of his career, though he developed some patterns more fully than others. When he found anything that he thought was one of his "bests," he used it again and again until it became stagnant and odious to the reader. His ideas might have been fresh in the first statement, but Carman lacked that powerful stabilizing tendency of mind which is present in major poets. A major poet is also aware of literary traditions, but he integrates these traditions into his poetry to create something new and vital.

Carman's poetry is permeated with strains of the American and English literary heritage, but the strongest is from the Romantic movement. His work can be called imitation, for there are obvious echoes. These patterns are present in his poetry from the time that he began to write until his death. At times he seems to slough off an influence, but though it disappears for a while, he comes back to it with a vital, and sometimes stronger, intensity. Never is a pattern forgotten; it is in the constant presence of the many patterns of Carman's poetry that his main charm lies. He chose his literary influences with care and at times he was more steeped in one than he was in another. These patterns, interwoven into Carman's poetry, form the bases of his style, thought, and content.

Carman was easily influenced by other people. His mother and George Parkin had persuaded him to go to Britain for a year after he graduated from the University of New Brunswick. Since he was, by his own admission, not a wanderer, he could not respond to Scotland and the Scots in a natural way. His response was, rather, superficial and sentimental. He commented on "the dourness of the people." This is the sort of cliché that Carman's response seems to endorse. He wrote to his mother, while studying at the University of Edinburgh:

For us who only want to know about a place for our own enjoyment, I expect the imagination of the place is better than the real knowledge.[3]

He had looked forward to his stay in Scotland and was disappointed when the reality did not live up to the expectation. His personality was dominantly Romantic, he was lonely, and his view of Edinburgh was that of a disillusioned Romantic idealist. He had gone to an ideal Scotland only to be dismayed by the reality. The bleakness of the city, and the windy and wet weather with little sun disappointed him. The Romantic temperament is often viewed as the predominance of imagination over reason, and with emphasis upon imaginative associations rather than upon direct objectivity. Carman's poetry is Romantic.

The tendency of Carman's personality to be predominantly Romantic can be easily explained. His formative years, the seventies and eighties of the last century, were spent when the reputations of the Romantic poets were high. The Victorian middle and upper classes, very conscious of poetry, considered the Romantic Movement the highest expression of poetry. Carman readily accepted this view of the Romantics. They were praised, and immediately Carman respected them all. He seems to have been incapable of a more intellectual approach to the values of the world around him. Arnold, the spokesman of the Victorians, praises Wordsworth, but rejects Keats' lack of "high seriousness." But Carman took the superficial view; he did not go into the core of things. At school, under Parkin, he soon became aware of the Romantics; his thought and personality were steeped in all the refinements of Romantic literature. The underlying assumptions of Romanticism became an intrinsic part of his thought and philosophy: a faith in the truth of instinct, a faith in creative imagination, a faith in the potentialities of the individual, a belief in a freedom which permits an individual to attain his destiny, a belief in the particular rather than the general, a belief in the value of new forms and style, an interest in the past, and an interest in nature combined with a deep communion with God.

His finest and purest gifts are Romantic. With appropriate and suggestive imagery, he creates mystery and melancholy; his nostalgic poetry is a product of slow and involved successions of sound combined with personal symbols. Carman's lyrics are best when he writes of nature:

> And there when lengthening twilights fall
> As softly as a wild bird's wing,
> Across the valley in the dusk
> I hear the silver flute of spring.
> ("The Flute of Spring")

A predominant note of "The Eavesdropper" (1893) is the imagery derived from nature:

> Outside, a yellow maple tree,
> Shifting upon the silvery blue
> With tiny multitudinous sound,
> Rustled to let the sunlight through.

Carman gained from William Wordsworth his fondness for nature. A love of 'natural' nature—nature unspoiled and unrestrained—had a special appeal for Carman and Wordsworth. Doubtless Carman himself knew what he thought of nature but Wordsworth's influence made him express himself as he did. Like Wordsworth, Carman reveled in the physical beauty of external nature; he worshipped, with intensity and vitality, the vivid loveliness of a budding tree, a blooming flower, and the inimitable sea. He attempted, as did Wordsworth, to liken man to nature and its phenomena:

> Was it a year or lives ago
> We took the grasses in our hands
> And caught the summer flying low
> Over the waving meadow lands,
> And held it there between our hands?
>
> The while the river at our feet—
> A drowsy inland meadow stream—
> At set of sun the after-heat
> Made running gold, and in the gleam
> We freed our birch upon the stream.
> ("Low Tide on Grand Pré")

Here is Wordsworth's contemplation and music, mingled with the wistfulness. Carman adopted the Wordsworthian philosophy that nature is good. He, too, held a similar belief in the essential goodness of man and nature and expressed it in the same way. Wordsworth saw God in nature:

> I heard among the solitary hills
> Low breathings coming after me, and sounds
> Of undistinguishable motion, steps
> Almost as silent as the turf they trod.
>
> ("The Prelude")

And so did Carman, for nature had given him a contemplative habit of mind:

> I took a day to search for God
> And found Him not. But as I trod
> By rocky ledge, through woods untamed
> Just where one scarlet lily flamed
> I saw His footprint in the sod.
>
> ("Vestigia")

This faith that God is in nature links the two poets.

Wordsworth's "I Wandered Lonely as a Cloud" seems to have had the most conspicuous influence upon Carman's verse; many stanzas show his debt to this poem. Today the poem has lost much of its freshness by reason of hackneyed recitations at school commencements, but to Carman, born in the 1860's, the poem had much of its original appeal. "The Dancers of the Field," 1895, is Wordsworthian in both tone and atmosphere:

> The wind went combing through the grass,
> The tall white daisies rocked and bowed;
> Such ecstasy as never was
> Possessed the shining multitude.

At once the poem brings Wordsworth's "golden daffodils ... fluttering and dancing in the breeze" to the reader's eye. And the poems end in similar ways; Wordsworth's "For oft, when on my couch I lie . . ." becomes:

> For I remembered like a dream
> How ages since my spirit flamed
> To wear their guise and dance with them.

This poem is completely modeled after the Wordsworth poem, except for the verse-form. The images of the flowers are retained until the last stanza in which reflection is used to tie the poem together and to give the picture of the past an essence of reality—though dream-like—in the present. Only the name of the flower is changed. And daisies grow wild in New Brunswick as do daffodils in England. He uses the poem as a source again in "Daisies":

> Over the shoulders and slopes of the dune
> I saw the white daisies go down to the sea.

This brings the Wordsworth image of:

> They stretched in never-ending line
> Along the margin of the bay:

The word "host," so original in Wordsworth, loses its connotations when Carman uses it again with the same emphasis at the beginning of the line "A host in the sunshine." Carman cannot be called, like his earlier fellow-Canadian Sangster, a true Wordsworthian poet, for he was too conscious of symbols in his nature poetry. He saw himself as part of nature:

> Between the roadside and the wood,
> Between the dawning and the dew
> A tiny flower before the sun,
> Ephemeral in time, I grew.
> ("Windflower")

Wordsworth used the flower as a symbol of nature, but his nature poetry was a summation of philosophy rather than true symbolism. Carman used nature, its growth and decay, symbolically, and he related his myth of man—birth, copulation, death—to nature and the seasons. Nature has a primal sexual significance for Carman. His most obvious sexual symbol related to nature appears in:

> Now the tulip lifts her chalice
> And the hyacinth his spear.
>   ("Resurgam")

Spring and rebirth bring the poem to a symbolic climax:

> Lo, now comes the April pageant
> And the Easter of the year.

Wordsworthian melancholy is transcendent in Carman's poetry. It is not maudlin, with excessive tears, but is close to fatalism. Wordsworth was conscious of a death which hovered continuously over man. He saw man as a part of nature that would by death and decay come to belong to the harmony of the universe. Carman reached this conclusion in "Windflower." It is Carman who believed, as the arch-Romantic of the twentieth century Dylan Thomas believed, that mankind is "green and dying"; death is so constantly with man, that even while he lives he is dying:

> Tonight can bring no healing now;
> The calm of yesternight is gone;
> Surely the wind is but the wind,
> And I a broken waif thereon.
>   ("Windflower")

Carman does not extend the didactic element in nature. Nature as teacher emerges only as a general impression from Carman's poetry. For when Carman realized that the flower had more than a symbolic or allegoric meaning, he saw its own intrinsic value:

> Let me have brook and flower and bird
> For counsellors, that I may learn
> The very accent of their tongue
> And its least syllable discern.

Wordsworthian child-like wonder is also present in Carman's verse. Simplicity made Wordsworth great, and Carman also delights in simple things. His images and his words are simple, but apt; the style is quiet and sober and occasionally rises to greatness.

But Carman sees Wordsworth superficially; he does not see his range, not even the emotional force of passages of *The Prelude* or the "Immortality" ode. He grasps only what he wants to see. Within his own limits, Carman is effective; though he is not great, he is sound; though he is not deeply philosophical, he has the wisdom of reflection.

Carman's verse differs from Coleridge's; the former's is diffuse, the latter's concentrated. The small output and frequently high level of Coleridge's poetry had an interesting effect on Carman's work, but the Canadian poet fell short. From "Kubla Khan" came Carman's interest in the impression of languid beauty lulled to emotional expression:

> The night has fallen, and the tide . . .
> Now and again comes drifting home,
> Across these aching barrens wide,
> A sigh like driven wind or foam:
> In grief the flood is bursting home.
> ("Low Tide on Grand Pré")

Carman used, too, the same vivid and yet unearthly colors; he mixed the actual expression of color in nature with brighter, more vivid, diction:

> Smolder and kindle and set fire
> To the dark selvedge of the night,
> The deep blue tapestry of stars,
> That sheet the dome in pearly light.
>
> . . . .
> High on a peak adrift with mist
> And round whose bases, far beneath
> The snow-white wheeling tropic birds,
> The emerald dragon breaks his teeth.
> ("A Seamark")

"A More Ancient Mariner," though in content and tone completely different from "The Rime of the Ancient Mariner," owes more than its title to Coleridge; the quatrain, with a rhyme of the second and fourth lines, is present also. Carman uses imagery here with a vitality which just escapes being truly like Coleridge in tone, as in:

> Who loves the booming wind in his ear

and

> Are shivered with fairy thunder

and

> He drones along with his rough sea-song

Although Carman lacked Coleridge's gift of compression and did not excel as a narrator, a number of his poems hover on the border-line between the ballad and fantasy ("The Nancy's Pride," "The Master of the Isles"); there is the terror and mystery of the northern coastline expressed with some of the intensity of a Coleridge:

> There is rumor in Dark Harbour,
> And the folk are all astir;
> For a stranger in the offing
> Draws them down to gaze at her,
>
> In the grey of early morning,
> Black against the orange streak,
> Making in below the ledges,
> With no colours at her peak.
>
> Something makes their hearts uneasy
> As they watch the long black hull,
> For she brings the storm behind her
> While before her there is lull.

Where Coleridge would create an atmosphere that "makes their hearts uneasy," Carman unskillfully has to tell his reader what emotion to feel. The poem reflects its model in the theme of death, and there is a fine blending of the form of an old ballad with the subject of modern life:

O Garvin! There is heartache
In tales that are half-told.

Carman weakened and often destroyed the mystical element, derived from Coleridge, by overwriting. He could not sustain the mystical penumbral quality of life present in the poetry of Coleridge, though he attempted frequently to do so.

The influences of Byron and Shelley are minor. From Byron Carman learned to describe gloom—Byronic gloom—with a beauty of verse and suggestive metaphor united with plaintive tone:

> My soul is dark—Oh quickly string
> The harp I yet can brook to hear
> ("My Soul is Dark")

At times Carman tried to gain Shelley's sense of aspiration, but his poetry lacks the sense of cosmic grandeur which Shelley's at its best can convey. Occasionally he almost succeeded:

> When the black horses from the house of Dis
> Stop at my door and the dread charioteer
> Knocks at my portal, summoning me to go
> On the far solitary unknown way
> Where all the race of me fare and are lost,
> Fleeting and numerous as the autumnal leaves
> Before the wind in Lesbos of the Isles;
>
> Though a chill draught of fear may quell my soul
> And dim my spirit like a flickering lamp
> In the great gusty hall of some old king,
> Only one mordant unassuaged regret,
> One passionate eternal human grief,
> Would wring my heart with bitterness and tears
> And set the mask of sorrow on my face.
> ("At The Great Release")

This poem gives the same impression of emotional intensity combined with logical incoherence that Shelley's verse often gives; it is as intense as Shelley's work, although it lacks his simplicity and variety. The run-on lines, the double adjectives ("mordant unassuaged," "passionate eternal"), the profusion of images ("black horses," "dread charioteer"), are all reminiscent of Shelley.

In Carman's love poetry there is an elevated mysticism expressed in fire and light images remindful of Shelley's love lyrics:

> I loved you when the tide of prayer
> Swept over you, and kneeling there
> In the pale summer of the stars,
> You laid your cheek to mine.
>
> I loved you when the auroral fire,
> Like the world's veriest desire,
> Burned up, and as it touched the sea,
> You laid your limbs to mine.
> (LIX, *Songs of the Sea Children*)

And "Spring Song" combines sensual feeling and fancy; this poem, too long in its original form, is full of Shelley's vigor, mingled with swift, light turns and a breathless running rhythm that carries the illustrating images with ease. In this one poem Carman's air of perfervid emotionalism approximates Shelley's.

Significantly, "The White Gull," (1892), Carman's most ambitious elegiac poem, laments the death of Shelley. In this poem, Carman's high imaginative vision captures and suggests Shelley's personality. The shining flight of the bird upon the horizon of the wide sea images Shelley's career as a poet. There is a buoyancy in the opening lines—buoyancy is a constant quality in Carman— which impressively strikes the keynote of his theme:

> Up by the idling reef-set bell
> The tide comes in;
> And to the idle heart to-day
> The wind has many things to say;
> The sea has many a tale to tell
> His younger kin.

The confused images and flaming epithets of the poem are far from logical, but by their very lack of logic they mirror the restless spirit of Shelley. Carman's profusion of similes—soul, pilgrim, gull

—denotes the ever-changing moods of Shelley. Carman saw Shelley as the leader of humanity in its great war for freedom:

> Oh, captain of the rebel host,
> Lead forth and far!
> Thy toiling troopers of the night
> Press on the unavailing flight;
> The sombre field is not yet lost,
> With thee for star.

He recognized Shelley as the leader of humanity in its Promethean struggle, and with short line verse-endings he echoed one of the favorite mannerisms of the Promethean Shelley, as in "Put scorn to scorn," and "From sea to sea."

Shelley's poetry is distinguished by its soaring quality, and "The White Gull" captures this effect. At times the colorful quality of Shelley's poetry is attained. The whole poem is permeated with the atmosphere and poetic devices of Shelley, as one stanza in particular illustrates:

> The gray sea-horses troop and roam;
> The shadows fly
> Along the wind-floor at their heels
> And where the golden daylight wheels,
> A white gull searches the blue dome
> With keening eye.

Archibald Lampman once said that Carman preferred to "steep his reader's imagination in splendid moods through the agency of magnificent metrical effects and a vast and mysterious imagery created under the presence of Beauty." [4] The same could be said of Keats. And it is to Keats that Carman owes his greatest debt. Carman, too, had "stood tiptoe upon a little hill" and had been moved by nature to create. The marriage of man and nature could originate a world of goodness and harmony, and Carman sought to symbolize this harmony in his poetry. He searched for beauty, and found it, as Keats had, in nature.

Carman, as did Keats, indulged in the "pathetic fallacy." In "Low Tide on Grand Pré" he makes nature bear the burden of his own emotion:

> A sigh like driven wind or foam:
> In grief the flood is bursting home.

Opulence of epithet and beauty of phrase completely dominate much of Carman's verse, as in:

> Low, now far on the hills
> The crimson fumes uncurled
> Where the caldron mantels and spills
> Another dawn on the world!
> ("A Northern Vigil")

and

> And the lonely spirit thrills
> To see the frosty asters like smoke upon the hills.
> ("An Autumn Song")

As in the work of Keats, alliteration and assonance are everywhere apparent. Here Carman uses sound to create atmosphere. The choice of vowel sounds was undoubtedly unconscious for both poets, but Carman's pursuit of assonance can be related to his reading and appreciation of John Keats.[5]

Possibly, too, the undercurrent of melancholy present in Carman's verse owes much to Keats. This note, originally heard in his first volume, *Low Tide on Grand Pré* (1893), was to occur in most of his verse. He sang sad songs of absent women, of unrest, of the futility of striving, and of the Arcadian gardens where love and dreams could be realized. His epitaph, perhaps, best exemplifies the melancholy of his poetry:

> Have little care that life is brief,
> And less that art is long;
> Success is in the silences,
> Though fame is in the song.
> ("Envoi")

Although Carman is sometimes vague when he speaks of nature, his images are often concrete and specific. Flowers, for example, are never merely flowers, nor trees only trees; they are always definite species—a marigold, a daisy, a scarlet maple, a silver birch. And a wind, or any aspect of nature, is always quali-fied by an adjective in an attempt, often successful, to give it a greater tangibility. Carman tries, like Keats, to present the con-crete image, to "load every rift with ore":

> Where the long winds stream and stream
> Clear across the dim blue distance
> Like a horn blown in a dream.
> ("The Grave-Tree")

> Soon we shall see the red vines ramp
> Through forest borders,
> And Indian summer breaking camp
> To silent orders.
> ("At Michaelmas")

The Keatsian qualities—those of predominant colors, love of beauty, and poignancy—are salient influences upon Carman's poetry. He recognizes his debt to Keats in another memorial poem, "By the Aurelian Wall":

> And so his splendid name,
> Who left the book of lyrics and small fame
> Among his fellows then,
> Spreads through the world like autumn—who
>   knows when?—
> Till all the hillsides flame.

Keats possessed certain Romantic qualities which are reflected in Carman's verse—the reawakened love of nature, the vitality of creative imagination, and a distinct, if not impressive, individual-ism. Carman looked back respectfully to Keats, as Keats himself had looked back to Chaucer, Spenser, the Elizabethans, and Mil-ton. For Keats had added his own individual thrust to the Roman-tic Movement—a vital interest in the traditions of English litera-ture. Carman was only too conscious of the Keats ode:

> How many bards gild the lapses of time!
> A few of them have ever been the food

> Of my delighted fancy—I could brood
> Over their beauties, earthly, or sublime:
> And, often, when I sit me down to rhyme,
> These will in throngs before my mind intrude:
> But no confusion, no disturbance rude
> Do they occasion; 'tis a pleasing chime.
> ("How Many Bards Gild the Lapses of Time")

Carman could only accept; his traditional training prevented his attempting new forms and themes.

Carman's greatest debt is to the Romantics. His rural background in the Maritimes and his home environment produced a temperament which can in part be compared with those of the great Romantics. His education made his poetic values coincide with theirs. All his life he was conscious of his own similarities to them, and he attempted to fuse their influences in his own poetry. He was separated by over half a century from them and limited by the standards of a different continent, but like the Romantics, Carman was a poet whose prime inspiration was nature; in this respect he fulfilled his desire to continue and enlarge the Romantic tradition in Canadian poetry.

Woven into the pattern of Carman's poetry is a marked characteristic of the Victorian age—moral purpose. Carman was brought up in an environment which accepted the Victorian values, a society which demanded that any creative work should justify its own existence by having a definite moral significance. Desmond Pacey has referred to Carman's thought as a "peculiarly jumbled version of the Victorian compromise." [6] Pacey continues:

The evil in the world is only apparent and temporary ("Evil is a dissonance, not a discord . . . Soon to be resolved in a happier phrase"); if Man will put himself in rhythmic harmony with Nature all will be well with him ("let the punctual tides instruct thee, and the planets give thee poise"); we should gratify the sense because that is the true means to spiritual enrichment ("Slake the sense now, that soul hereafter . . . Go not forth a starved defrauding thing"). [7]

Carman was deeply aware of the great Victorians—Tennyson, Browning, Arnold, Carlyle, Ruskin—who were teachers of society with faith in their message and a conscious purpose to uplift and instruct. But his concept of the Victorian ideal is limited by his own vision of it. He was unable to see that the Victorian compromise is very much a myth, and his philosophy of man and nature hardly agrees with that of Arnold, the high-priest of Victorian cultural values who, like Tennyson saw man and nature in perpetual conflict. So often Carman was unable to extend his thinking beyond mediocrity; perhaps he did not have the intelligence to do so.

Tennyson died the year before Carman's first book of poetry, *Low Tide on Grand Pré* (1893), was published. Up to that time, and throughout the entire Victorian period, Tennyson stood on the pinnacle of poetry in England; he was the voice of an age, expressing its doubts and faiths, griefs and triumphs. Carman's letters do not mention Tennyson, but no young man with any pretensions to literary culture—however insincere or affected he might be—growing up in the sixties and seventies of the last century, could fail to have read Tennyson. For direct evidence that he had, there is a parody of "Crossing the Bar," written in 1895. Carman used the rhythms of that poem as a direct model, but created a comic effect quite different from the original. Here the spontaneity comes from both Tennyson and Carman, and is probably Carman at his most sincere, post-graduate student best:

> Sunset and good cigar
>   And a great thirst in me;
> And may my friends be loafing at the bar
>   When I go in to see.
>
> . . . .
>
> And though within this bright seductive place
>   My dollars go not far,
> I never more shall see them face to face
>   When they have crossed the bar.

Tennyson was an artist who studied the art of poetry with a singleness of purpose. Because of this study, he had few rivals in melody and the perfect finish of his verse.[8] He was conscious of the musical quality of poetry and wrought his stanzas with full attention to cadence and rhythm. He was conscious, too, of atmosphere, and suited his choice of sounds and words to the intended mood. Like all Victorian poets, he was emphatically a teacher. His theme was the reign of order in the world which would produce the perfect man. In three distinctly different poems—*In Memoriam, Idylls of the King, The Princess*—the main theme is an ordering development of law in both the spiritual and natural world. But though Tennyson's overt philosophy was optimistic and progressive, his chief emotional tone, as W. H. Auden has brilliantly demonstrated, was melancholy.[9] His life had been clouded by the death of his close friend, Arthur Hallam, and he brought to his poetry a quality of despondency, a loss of hope in life and mankind, which his surface optimism only thinly disguised.

Unfortunately, Carman did not possess in full measure Tennyson's artistic conscience. He did not have Tennyson's capacity for working out the flaws in his poems, either because he did not recognize them, or because he was too impatient to make a satisfactory change. However, he did try to attain the Tennysonian quality of rhythm and musical cadences. Often he succeeded, for his best poems ("Low Tide on Grand Pré," "The Windflower," "Noons of Poppy") are his best because of their Tennysonian qualities of song and cadence. In "Noons of Poppy," the singing rhythm captures all the characteristics of Tennyson's "Blow Bugle Blow." Where Tennyson uses the *o* and *e* for the rolling quality, Carman too has experimented with vowel sounds to give a poem a song-like intensity. Note the *o* (noon, of, poppy, love, above), The *a* and *e* (scarlet, acres, sea, theme), and the soft *u* and *v* (burning, full, blue, above, love):

> Noons of poppy, noon of poppy,
> Scarlet acres by the sea
> Burning to the blue above them,
> Love, the world is full for me.

Tennyson was also an inspiration to Carman in methods of description and atmosphere creation. The complete volume, *Low Tide on Grand Pré*, evokes the mood of loss and vague regret that Tennyson so often captures. The poet's personal grief is reflected in the wanderings of the river:

> A grievous stream, that to and fro
> Athrough the fields of Acadie

Goes wandering, as if to know
Why one beloved face should be
So long from home and Acadie.

Almost all of Carman's early poetry has this quality of despair;
even in his late, and predominantly more optimistic verse, it is
occasionally present. In "A Song Before Sailing," he says:

Blow me beyond the grime
And pestilence of time!
I am too sick at heart to war
With failure anymore.

In the last verse of the poem, the atmosphere is even more akin to
that of Tennyson's work:

Wind of the dead men's feet,
Blow through the empty street;
The last adventurer am I,
Then, world, goodbye!

When he desires to evoke this atmosphere, Carman often chooses
the quatrain, the stanza form used by Tennyson in *In Memoriam*
and other poems of the same tone. This verse form had been used
with greatest success by Tennyson, and Carman, in using it to
create the same mood, acknowledges his debt to Tennyson. The
melancholy note is heard dominantly in his early poems, but occasionally throughout his life. Carman came to feel and say that one
should deal not only with the unhappy, but also with happy
moments. The Tennysonian influence is an early influence;
Browning's optimism and his own little Mary Perry King made
Carman change his mind and determine to be a happy writer, an
artist of joy.

Carman uses the same rich coloring and descriptive images that
Tennyson uses in his poems, particularly "St. Agnes' Eve":

The scarlet of the maples can shake me like a cry
Of bugles going by.
And my lonely spirit thrills

> To see the frosty asters like smoke upon the hills.
> ("An Autumn Song")

If Tennyson was an inspiration to Carman in methods of description and the evocation of atmosphere, he was also a source for didacticism and moralism. Carman reached toward Tennyson's emphatic tone as a teacher. He saw, as Tennyson had seen, that perfect man was a result of a reign of order. He was a traditionalist in politics and looked back to the past for an order which could come out of a faith in that past. Skeptical about the progress of his own society, he shared Tennyson's fear of democracy in politics:

> We have scorned the belief of our fathers
> And cast their quiet aside;
> To take the mob for our ruler
> And the voice of the mob for our guide.
> ("Twilight in Eden")

He saw a quality of hectic, almost unhealthy, turmoil in the men of his time who were experimenting with new ideas and philosophies:

> New art, new movements, and new schools,
> Ill maimed and blind and halt.
> ("A Spring Feeling")

This attitude is similar to Tennyson's in "Locksley Hall Sixty Years After," and appears in Arnold's work. But Tennyson frequently assumed the role of prophet; Carman seldom did. His poetry and his friends were his life, and he was content to leave the social and political problems of his time in abler hands. Carman was much less vitally interested than Tennyson in public issues.

Carman believed with Tennyson that the supreme purpose of the laws of nature and mankind was to be a revelation of love. He accepted Tennyson's message that, because law and love are in the world, faith is the only possible human response, even though there is no logical way to demonstrate its validity. Carman's ideal was love; his continual acceptance of it as life's supreme value enlarged it into a widening concept—love of beauty, love of nature, and love of friends—that became the beginning and end of his creed.

But it is to Robert Browning that Carman owes the greatest debt, though he did not fully appreciate Browning or completely understand his ideas. He saw Browning, rather, as most Victorians did; his response to Browning is similar to that of the Victorian age, which needed the faith that Browning had. Carman could easily identify his concept of love as the ideal of ultimate felicity with Browning, or with any of the lyric idealists of the past. Carman saw Tennyson and Browning as poets in perfect accord, in one respect at least; he felt that each had found in love the supreme purpose and meaning of life. However, Tennyson is first the artist and then the teacher, while for Browning the message is always the important thing. Carman was unable to see that there is little "message" in "Love Among the Ruins" or "Two in the Campagna" and in many of the love lyrics. Carman considered Browning the teacher of the age, though Browning is always accused of turning his back on the social and moral questions of his day; Tennyson, really, is the spokesman of the age. Carman saw Browning in all the clichés of Browning criticism: the strength, the joy in life, the invincible optimism. The last particularly filled Carman's cup, and he forgot that Browning had said "the more of doubt, the more of faith." In the dramatic monologue, Browning wrote about the ugly and the beautiful with the same intensity and pleasure, and aimed to show that truth was present in both good and evil. Carman looked at the generalizations, not the specifics. For him, Browning's message was the triumph of the individual over all obstacles; self is not subordinate, but supreme. What set Browning's thought apart from that of his contemporaries was his sense of the challenge in life, the striving for the unattainable, the delight in the struggle. This energy, this cheerful courage, and his faith in life, appealed to Carman's manhood and growing maturity. So again it was the framework only that Carman was able to see; he seems to have difficulty distinguishing between the myth and reality in the writers of his own age; perhaps this is why so much of the legend of his own life was perpetrated by Carman himself. He seems to be ignorant of the essence of Browning; rather, he sees Browning as most people of his age wanted to see him, overlooking the intrinsic meanings of a man who could write to Ruskin that a poet's only obligation was to God, not to the world or society.

One of the first poems to show Browning's influence is "The Wanderer," where Browning's optimistic vigor is apparent in the anapestic lines:

> Therefore is joy more than sorrow, foreseeing
> The lust of the mind and the lure of the eye
> And the pride of the hand have their hour of triumph,
> But the dream of the heart will endure by-and-by.

He, too, saw the challenge in life and found joy in living because of the struggle involved:

> Come where the urge of desire availeth,
> And no fear follows the feet of the rain;
> ("The Wanderer")

There is positive statement that Carman was fond of the poetry of Browning. From Edinburgh in 1883, he wrote to his mother that he was again reading Browning's poetry:

I have learned a good deal from a new book I have, which has in it a study of Browning. There are so many new thoughts good and true.[10]

This lonely year intensified the Browning influence. "In a Copy of Browning," written in 1896, is a playful appreciation of Browning's character and poetry, acknowledging Carman's debt to Browning for the concept of love as a primal force:

> With you for teacher
> We learned love's feature
> In every creature
> That roves or grieves:
> When winds were brawling
> Or bird-folk calling
> Or leaf-folk falling
> About our eaves.

The debt of form is indicated by the concise run-on lines that gain in swiftness not only by their own run-on quality, but by their brevity:

> Since first I sought you,
> Found you and bought you
> Hugged you and brought you
> Home from Cornhill,
> While some upbraid you
> And some parade you,
> Nine years have made you
> My master still.

In *Behind the Arras* (1895), Carman achieves a much different style and tone from the soft, elegiac strain of his previous volume of poems, *Low Tide on Grand Pré*. Here the model is Browning; he uses the brisk pace and the metrical device of a long line in sharp contrast with a short one, which was a favorite of Browning. The idea that man is an imperfect creature, even an illogical one, and that he has a further destiny, is the same thought that is present in Browning's "Cleon." "Behind the Arras" is Carman's most complete effort in philosophical poetry. His allegory, at first, has the brillance of Browning, and because Carman was a poet with a passion for suggestion, the symbolical allegory is one of his favorite patterns. He is a disciple of Browning here and tries to approximate his master's art in fusing human drama with philosophical theory. Browning's monologues of the middle period evoke a modern spirit; since they shared a transcendental optimism, Carman used Browning's form when he wanted to express the same views. The monologue was a form in which Carman could feel at home, and he tried to use the casual descriptions with which Browning achieves his effect. These descriptions in Carman's work, however, fail to attain Browning's piquancy of manner. He was too fond of smoothly beautiful descriptions to achieve the sharpness of Browning's images.

In "Beyond the Gamut" (1895), Carman moves even closer to the dramatic style of Browning's monologues. He advocates the theme present in Browning's "Abt Vogler"—that from music comes the idea of the divine rhythm of the universe. Carman states:

> Man is but the morning dream of nature
> Roused by some wild cadence weird and strange.

For Carman there was the "Earth one habitat of spirit merely," reiterating Browning's belief in the greatness of heaven and the peace and calm of death:

> Lower me down from the slope of life, and leave me
> Knowing the hereafter will be well.

Unfortunately the frame of the dramatic monologue was too vast for Carman's mind. He lacked the intellect to give it a clear and logical development, or any really artistic unity. He could not create a picture of life and retain the sharp flavor which characterized Browning's monologues.

Songs From a Northern Garden (1904) is another attempt by Carman to write in a high didactic vein. When he writes in this manner he comes very much under Browning's influence. A particular poem in this volume, "Above the Gaspereau" (1897), shows the influence of Browning in all its facets. The metrical mold is the same as Browning's "The Englishman in Italy"; the flavor is the same:

> There are sunflowers too in my garden on top of the hill
> Where now in early September the sun has his will,—

He tried for Browning's familiarity with "Was that so important? Ah, yes," and the similar sense of observation, comprehensive and keen:

> Taste the apple, bite in to the juice; how abundant and sweet!

There are the same swift side glances:

> So much for mere fact, mere impressions. So much I portray
> Of the atmosphere, colour, illusion of one autumn day,

Browning's characteristic calls and apostrophes are maintained:

What is it? Who comes? What's abroad on the blue mountainside? . . .
You, Londoner, walking in Bishopsgate, strolling the Strand.

The whole poem has a vigor of invention which is like that of the original inspiration.

Browning also inspired the form and tone of "The Word at St. Kavin's." In style it can be compared to his "Rabbi Ben Ezra." The accented and unaccented syllables present in the iambic feet stress boldness and masculinity; the third and last lines of each stanza are lengthened to create a strengthening effect.

> Once at St. Kavin's door
> I rested. No sign more
> Of discontent escaped me from that day
> For there I overheard
> A Brother of the word
> Expound the grace of poverty and say: . . .

The philosophy expressed recognizes evolution but with a faith that this doctrine, though scientific, can be reconciled with the hopes of spiritual traditions. Unfortunately Carman did not have the weight of thought to support the extreme emphasis of the style.

It was easy for Carman to make Browning's manner his own. He recaptures Browning's vision and frequently the phrases have all the vigor of the master. Browning's narrative style, with its realistic and familiar scenes, is especially apparent in "The Man With the Tortoise" (1901), and "On The Plaza" (1900):

> One August day I sat beside
> A cafe window open wide
> To let the shower-freshened air
> Blow in across the Plaza, where
> In golden pomp against the dark
> Green leafy background of the Park
> St. Gauden's hero, gaunt and grim
> Rides on with Victory leading him.

Though the Victorian age is generally characterized as practical and materialistic, nearly all the writers, and especially the great poets, attacked materialism and exalted a purely idealistic concept of life. Carman saw Tennyson and Browning as fundamentally exemplary poets, with love, truth, brotherhood, and justice emphasized as the chief ends of life. He agreed with their ideas, and their poetry had a rapid and far-reaching effect on his own verse. At various times during Carman's career, Tennyson, Browning, and to a lesser extent, Arnold, laid a strong hand on Carman's poetry. These influences, however, were not sufficiently strong to make Carman their disciple or imitator. He assimilated certain ideas and qualities of style from them, but these trends were brought together with ideas from others and with his own ideas and style. His poetry, then, as a whole, is quite distinct from the poetry of either Tennyson or Browning.

Dr. Parkin drew Carman's attention to the works of the Pre-Raphaelites, who were exciting the literary world when Carman was in secondary school. There is evidence that Carman knew Rossetti in what Charles G. D. Roberts says about Dr. Parkin:

He would take us favoured two for long hikes over the wooded hills of Fredericton. England just then was thrilling to the new music, the new colour, the new raptures of Swinburne and Rossetti. Parkin would recite . . . above all "The Blessed Damozel," which he loved so passionately that Bliss suspected him of sometimes saying it in his prayers.[11]

Carman was aware of Rossetti and Swinburne—and also had a sense of humor.

Rossetti wrote some poetry of intellectual force; he gave a new life to the ballad in that he modified it into a cultured form; and though his rhythms are not very strong, he had a fine sense of words. His imagery is sumptuous and his "painted" pictures sensuous; the majority of his poems are almost overweighted with a profusion of descriptive details and suggestions. There is one group of poems which deals with medieval times in which he tried, through various forms, firmer attempts at dramatic narrative. Significantly, his return to nature is a return to nature as he saw it, not as Wordsworth saw it. Rather, the works of Rossetti and the Pre-Raphaelites are a mixture, with the natural profusion of Keats underlined by the symbolic suggestiveness of Shelley.

Rossetti has a medieval and archaic tendency and brings with this his predominant concept that an artist, whether painter or poet, must devote himself to expressing his own personal thoughts and that they, in turn, must be based upon a direct study of nature. For Rossetti, the life of the imagination created his poetry—as it creates all poetry—and it is mystical, full of passion, haunted by a sense of beauty, with an intense need of loving and being loved. It is genial, but dominantly weak, and has an ardent but impatient tone.

It is in Carman's love lyrics that the influence of Rossetti is most apparent. His metaphors have the Rossetti qualities of picture and suggestion; they are often illuminated:

> In the cold of the dawn I rose
> Life lay there from hill to hill
> In the core of a blue pearl,
> As it seemed, so deep and still.
> (XXVIII, *Songs of the Sea Children*)

He follows Rossetti's extensive use of color words to create mood. While Rossetti's words are usually applied to physical descriptions or room furnishings, Carman's colors are used for external nature. But he applies the medieval color words of Rossetti here; he uses words like "golden," which Rossetti liked frequently to use in his descriptions of medieval rooms. Carman follows Rossetti in an over-indulgence in detailed descriptions. Often his many pictures, while apt, are too heavy for his verse. In "Eyes Like Summer After Sundown" the tone is Rossetti's, and the images have the concrete quality which Rossetti achieved in "The Blessed Damozel":

> Eyes like summer after sundown,
> Hands like roses after dew,
> Lyric as a blown rose garden
> The wind wanders through.
>
> Swelling breasts that bud to crimson,
> Hair like cobwebs after dawn,
> And the rosy mouth wind-riffled
> When the wind is gone.

This poem is marred by the image of "hair like cobwebs after dawn"—it is Carman at his worst—though it is not as bad, surely, as Rossetti's famous image, "Her hair that lay along her back / Was yellow like ripe corn." The sensuous quality of "The Blessed Damozel" is found in many of the lyrics in *Songs of the Sea Children* (1904), and in many of Carman's ballads:

> Then came a glimmering of white—
> The drench of sheer diaphanous lawn,
> More palpable than light of stars,
> And more delectable than dawn.
>   (LXII, *Songs of the Sea Children*)

Carman does not write the archaic and medieval poetry in which Rossetti delighted. When not discussing his immediate world of nature and love, he writes of Pan and his contemporaries and relates this subject to his own immediate scene. Where Rossetti chose medieval legends with which to fuse his own ideals, Carman looked back farther and wrote of Syrinx and her transformation into the "magic flute" of Pan. He wrought these poems with Rossetti's longing for love, but the sensual pictures of physical beauty are absent. He does not describe physical beauty as Rossetti did in his poetry; with Carman there is only a phrase description, as in:

> Where some lithe Bithynaian flute-boy, nude and
>   golden in the sun,
>   ("Syrinx")

And at times he uses several words ("dark Peruvian lover," "a young herdsman golden haired"—too often he seems interested only in physical descriptions of young, well-built men) but never is there a complete stanza of physical description except when Carman's sense of humor is evident:

> My glorious enchantress,
> She went with silken hose,
> With swaying hip and curving lip
> And little tilted nose.
>   ("The Enchantress")

Here is the facetious Carman. He does not seem to be concerned with integrating a sensual picture into his verse. He was too shy and reserved—and introverted, as can be seen by his letters—to be sincere in a sensual poem, and he used humor to escape from his personal embarrassment.

Carman's poetry has most of the Rossetti qualities of atmosphere: melancholy, passion, mysticism, reciprocated love. But Rossetti is a late Romantic, and few of his ideas were new or striking. Rossetti's poetry influenced Carman in that it strengthened his impulse to be Romantic in the sense that Keats and Shelley were Romantic.

Two other figures of the Pre-Raphaelite movement—Christina Rossetti and William Morris—had a minor, but genuine, effect on Carman's poetry. There is no indication in Carman's letters or books that he admired or condemned the work of these two writers, but it can be assumed that because of his "traditional" schooling, Carman was conscious of his contemporaries. From Christina Rossetti Carman borrowed the careful workmanship and exquisite melody so evident in some of his short lyrics; he learned from her the rule of compression, and it is in the short lyrics that his greatest poetic effects are made. Christina Rossetti's work is marked, too, by her personality; she was a sincere, affectionate person whose life was regulated by her religion, and her tenderness and sincerity are evident in her poems.

It is this sincerity which links Carman's poetry to Christina Rossetti's. Carman's poetry has a minor theme, but it never lacks a genuine tenderness and it is continually sincere. It was his nature to embrace sincerity, and it lacks a masculine gusto; it is a feminine sincerity much like the poignancy of Christina Rossetti:

> When the great storm out of dark shall drive
> And blur the sun, and bugle my release,
> Let not thy weary earthling faint nor strive,
> Faring beyond the tumult to thy peace.
> ("The Great Return")

Carman echoed Christina Rossetti's method of using simple rhyme, rhythm, and singing melody to create a mood.

In many ways William Morris in his early phase is more typical of the Pre-Raphaelite Brotherhood than is Christina Rossetti. His medieval poems have a reality which similar work of the century lacks. The lyrics of Morris have a spontaneous quality, and he loaded them with many pictures so that the strength is not in the pictures separately, but in the cumulative impression which they create. Unfortunately, his main fault is too much fluency, and the intensity of his poetry is watered down with excessive words. Much can be said about Carman in the same way. There is energy and force, but the recurrent themes are the beauty of life, the fleetingness of love, and the inevitability of death. These are the qualities of his first phase.

It is this first phase which Carman often approximates in his own poetry. Although he seldom uses a medieval setting, Carman often creates an atmosphere which appears medieval. His ballads are an example of this, and in them a Morris tone is achieved:

> The scarlet fruit will come to fill,
> The scarlet spring to stir
> The golden rowan of Menalowan,
> And wake no dream for her.

Although the main quality of the ballads is more like that of Coleridge, traces of Morris' works are present. The resemblance here is in tone; both have the same spontaneous quality in their verse and both suffer from the use of too many words, which weaken the vitality of their poetry. Both share the same vein of sadness which is wistful, but never plangent. This recurrence of melancholy in Morris and Carman was a product of their respective ages and environments. Morris, in his late phase, was at odds with his capitalistic society and though Carman never felt out of tune with his environment (except at Edinburgh), both poets possess with intensity, the sense of the shortness of life and love. Whatever reservations may be made as to the poetry of both men, it does make agreeable reading. The similarity of the two poets gives the general impression that Morris' poetry was a minor influence on Carman's verse.

Carman's poetry is only occasionally Pre-Raphaelite, and when it is, it is more a blending of Keats, Rossetti, and Carman's own distinctive application of the influences. From the Pre-Raphaelite

Brotherhood, Carman assimilated a musical quality, a richness of color, and a reaffirmation of the Keatsian love of beauty. The Pre-Raphaelites strengthened his interest in the first Romantics and so, from the last Romantics, Carman created a poetry which is, for the most part, Romantic in style, thought, and tone.

Of the minor influences, the one of Robert Louis Stevenson is the most obvious. Stevenson was the inspiration for the three *Vagabondia* volumes, for Carman saw in him the epitome of a man who had the wanderlust. Both poets wrote of the wanderer in an ideal mood, for they did not have the physical strength to pursue this life in reality and, instead, wrote poems celebrating it. He borrowed the simple, direct approach from Stevenson in these volumes, and also in other poems captures the quality of Stevenson's *A Child's Garden of Verses*. This is especially noticeable in "The Ships of Yule" which resembles Stevenson's "Block City" in atmosphere and thought. Where Stevenson conjured up countries and cities out of his blocks, Carman envisaged trips for his toy ships. They both look back to childhood with happy memories, as a comparison of the last verses of the two poems shows:

> And even after I was big
> And had to go to school,
> My mind was often far away
> Aboard my Ships of Yule.
> —Carman

> Yet as I saw it, I see it again,
> The kirk and the palace, the ships and the men,
> And as long as I live and where'er I may be,
> I'll always remember my town by the sea.
> —Stevenson

Carman also borrowed atmosphere from Elizabeth Barrett Browning, Edward Fitzgerald, and the Decadents; what he is really doing when he imitates these poets is capturing the taste of the time. If he knew that one quality was popular, he tried to copy it. Often, then, influences appear more to reveal Carman as a product of his time rather than as a deliberate copier. But his product is never new; he was so highly imitative that many influences from poets of the nineteenth century converge in his work. On occasion these influences can be traced to a set of lines; more often they are evident by tonal effects and thought sequences. There is the "vagabondia" of Stevenson, the preoccupation with extreme emotion of the Decadents, the love lyrics of Elizabeth Barrett Browning, the Persian imagery of Edward Fitzgerald, and the paganism of Swinburne—all at a lesser intensity than in the originals that provided the inspiration.

Because Carman's poetry is so predominantly nineteenth-century in tone, he was greatly influenced by the major poets of that time. But because there are similarities between his work and that of an earlier poet, can the reader always assume that there is a definite link between the two? Some of the similarity is chiefly the result of the same background, education, and values; often, perhaps, the similarities are not the result of influences, but rather the result of the same attitude to life and poetic values. It is clear that neither explanation is complete in itself; each has its own relevance under different conditions.

If a writer has never read a certain work, any similarity that may be evident is clearly only an approximation of thought and style. However, if the poet has read certain works, they have a definite place and form—however subtle this may be—in the evolution of his own style. The imitation of models was a mainstay of nineteenth-century education. Assimilation is the most evasive influence to determine and discuss, but in spite of this and because of its pervasive nature, it is perhaps the most important. Assimilation is seldom a conscious thing, and only in various "passings" may a reader note the poet's acknowledgement of his debt to the thought and style of other writers. With Carman, to determine an influence is not always quite so difficult as it is with other writers. In a number of instances, there are Carman's own comments which show his interest in the poets of the nineteenth century; in others, he is very obviously reflecting certain stylistic devices and attitudes of other poets; in still others there are the versified tributes to those poets whom he most admired—a sure indication that his admiration of them was not entirely superficial and occasional —for Carman was frequently more sincere than good as a poet. Above all, the presence of influences is attested by the fact that

Carman was a traditionalist in poetry, rather than an innovator as were Wordsworth, Rossetti and Swinburne. He really brought nothing new to poetry, and sought only to bring together his own favorite expressions in poetry which seemed to suit his limited emotional and intellectual view of life.

CHAPTER 5

Conclusion

CARMAN'S whole attitude to poetry was that of the devotee rather than a true creator. He worshipped at the shrine but was never able to penetrate to the inner circle; his was a minor inspiration because of the narrow range of subject matter and mood. Had Carman been a truly original poet, he would have shown a development toward a greater assurance of style and a deeper emotional and intellectual content. However, between the early Carman and the late Carman the differences are in minor tones and in the fact that, for a time, one idea is predominant over others. For a while one may believe that there is a development, but always he returns to something he had pursued before. There is no sign of growth as in Keats, no strongly conscious change as in Yeats. Carman's outlook and attitude changed very little from the beginning to the end of his work.

Even though his themes are limited, he was able for the most part to give a spontaneous quality to his verse; and even when he is at his most original there is an innate respect for the traditional standards and values of English poetry. A poet like Carman could only look back to the past. Among several characteristics linking him with strong tendencies in the work of nineteenth-century poets is his pervading melancholy—the sweet sadness of the transience of love and of life which is akin to the sadness of Keats, Christina Rossetti, and Ernest Dowson. His melancholy is more diffuse than theirs; it is a mood rather than a view of life. When he wrote in the melancholy strain, he showed that the influence of these poets was upon him, for the general tone is so closely related that it becomes an influence rather than a resemblance based upon the same ideas and values. This melancholy is an intrinsic part of his early poetry.

A counter-quality, found frequently in his later poetry, is the optimism which he derived in part from the Unitrinianism of Mrs. Mary Perry King. There is always a possibility of harmony within the universe, a harmony of the body, spirit and the mind. This harmony comes when man respects himself and his environment, grasping the potential for strength and contentment by balancing all his mental and physical power. At times, his optimism comes from the American euphemism of the sunny smile (in the face of pain and sorrow); this came to him after he had left behind him the loves and youthful sadness he associated with his life in New Brunswick. But Carman was always an optimist; in the early part of his career he affected a melancholy because he thought it was expected of young poets; maybe it is.

But in both his sad and optimistic poetry one theme pervades—a sentimental emotionalism. His sincere and humble personality could accept this since he lacked any strongly mature stabilizing factor of mind. This emotional quality has a certain charm and poignancy characteristic of his age and at the same time is the result of the simplicity of his personality. Carman's chief human values were centered in strong personal attachments; his was a personality which needed to give and receive affection. He needed the security that friends give. He needed to be able to predict reactions in people around him; Mary Perry King was able to give him an anchor in life because she was consistent. Carman always felt at home in her company. This was the one thing that was most important to Carman: to find stability and predictability in the world around him. Because he strove so much for this quality in his personal life, paradoxically his poetry lacks a stabilizing factor, something which ties it together. No core is ever found; nothing is forever in the poetry of Bliss Carman. It flares up, burns away, and then is gone!

Carman's reliance on people to sustain him brings about his interest in the natural world around him. He was fond of this world, and the background and imagery of his poetry is derived almost wholly from nature. In this he is a true follower of Wordsworth; he has the same childlike fascination with simple description, and his diction is usually of almost austere simplicity. He saw everything in terms of nature. The connecting link in his poetry is seasonal; he correlates emotion to either spring, summer, autumn or winter. Spring is most meaningful to him; it has the associations of awakening and freshness, of new greenery, or more powerful tides. He creates mood by using the natural phenomena of nature. All the world is seen through nature as a heightening dimension; personal relationships are consistently framed in a natural setting. His colors and imagery, too, are derived from this central theme. There is little classical, Christian, or literary imagery in his work. Even in the *Pipes of Pan* series, the source of word-pictures and music is the world of nature. Such word combinations as "gold-green shadows," "soft purple haze," "pale aster-blue" are frequently present, and show his tendency to represent his ideas in terms closely related to natural phenomena.

He goes to music, too, for the rhythms in his work; he is the "harp-string in the wind." Carman felt, quite obviously, that poetry should be like music. Many of his poems have a musical rhythm, and a few have been set to music ("Vestigia," "Ships of Yule"). But Carman did not create any new dimension in musical poetry as did Verlaine, nor did he approximate Wagner who had created a new music. His images do not possess any abstract value like musical notes and chords; they are rather musical because they sing of simple, individual emotions which can be related to the folk-song type of music. Occasionally he created poems which seem to be deliberately musical. In "The Ghostyard of the Gold-enrod" he employed words with extreme care and set them to reflect an atmosphere. There is, in this poem, the wandering and elusive qualities of the music of Debussy, a delicate and stealthful use of words with an almost timid precaution:

> When the first silent frost has trod,
> The ghostyard of the goldenrod,
>
> And laid the blight of his cold hand
> Upon the warm autumnal land,
>
> And all things wait the subtle change
> That men call death, is it not strange
>
> That I—without a care or need,
> Who only am an idle weed—
>
> Should wait unmoved, so frail, so bold,
> The coming of the final cold.

Here he was guided by rhythm and his theme is finely shaped; the poem is so well worked over that the finished product cannot be recognized as characteristically Carman's. For the most part, his music is simple rhythms, controlled by end rhymes; he lets the classical lyric and the ballad serve as models for the rhythm and flow of his work.

The story of Bliss Carman—his poetry and his life—is incontestably and peculiarly Canadian. He had to go to the United States to achieve his reputation; only after he had succeeded there would his own countrymen recognize him. In fact, he had to become seriously ill before the critics and his fellow-poets began to praise him. This happens so often in the history of Canadian letters, for the Canadian public is never sure of its reactions to its own artists and writers. There is often an apologetic quality about the presence of the artist in the Canadian society; if the rest of the world acclaims him then the Canadian public reinforces the acclaim, but its impetus must come from elsewhere. If the rest of the world was willing to recognize a strong talent in Carman, then Canadians were willing to admit it also; they were, in fact, willing to create the image of a Canadian poet who was much greater in stature than Carman actually was.

Carman's literary reputation reached its high point at the beginning of his career, when *Low Tide on Grand Pré* was published in 1894. For the next ten years his public sustained the reputation that the book had established, even though the poems published in this period were weak in comparison to the ones of 1894. His critical reputation continued to be strengthened by what he had done in the past rather than what he was doing in the present. From 1910 until Carman's death in 1929 his critical reputation changed little. It was as though critics were afraid to say what they thought of his new verse because they hoped that the next volume would match the beauty of the earlier lyrics. His friends were his critics; they knew of his poet-in-waiting relationship with Mary Perry King, and they thought it harmed his writing. But if they criticized his work she would, perhaps, hold him even closer, away from the harsh world that did not like his work. The critics played a waiting game, and they waited in vain.

In the early twenties Carman continued to hold his high place in Canadian literature. Many considered him the originator of a new school, along with Charles G. D. Roberts; though his imitators had surpassed the innovator, Carman retained a high position in recognition of his services to Canadian letters. He held a kind of father-figure position, and no one would tarnish the picture. The Maritimes held onto its local loyalty to Carman, and as yet Ontario had not produced anyone as good as Carman, or at least anyone as well known. In 1923 Odell Shepard published his book, *Bliss Carman*, and it was a reverent work written by a man who knew his subject well, and loved the man and the legend. Carman had almost died in 1921; it was felt that any unfavorably critical opinion might bring about a relapse. Furthermore, the Canadian public would disapprove such treatment.

Carman died in 1929, and James Cappon's book on Carman came out the following year; the book was ready for the press before Carman's death, and though Cappon makes some reference as an appendix to the book about Carman's "recent death," the book does attempt the occasional honest criticism of Carman as a writer. As a man of position in Canadian letters, Cappon was able to see the large influence Carman had wielded, and Cappon esteemed this; in a sense he was guided more by the myth than by the poetry itself. Elegies to Carman followed Cappon's book; the legend intensified itself in the decade to follow. Carman was considered a great writer but he was out of fashion in the thirties; poets such as Earle Birney, E. J. Pratt, and Dorothy Livesay did not imitate Carman, but they also were aware that Carman had paved the way for them. Carman had opened many doors for the Canadian poet; it often seems that the critics were afraid to level any criticism at the poet who had awakened the Canadian audience.

But the time came for the reappraisals, and gradually Carman lost favor with his fellow-poets, the poets who followed him. But often, rather than condemn or criticize him, they avoided a direct evaluation by putting him into a niche as the leader of the sixties group of poets, and leaving him there. They did not like his poetry, but it was not Carman's fault; the times had changed, and so "for his own time" Carman was an effective poet. But still, the question of a full evaluation was avoided. When the Canadian critic learned that he did not have to defend his taste, or categorize historically the artistic products of his own country, Carman received a more complete, and a more sincere criticism. The legend persisted that he had done a great service to Canadian poetry—and this he did do—but his work was minor, with occasional glows of brilliance.

After the war, and more particularly in 1950 with Desmond Pacey's reappraisal in the *Northern Review,* Carman's reputation began to crystallize even more. Most critics rejected him as a very minor voice; Pacey in a sense agreed, but he saw the minor voice as one that had a strong position in Canadian poetry and one which had produced the finest lines of poetry of his time. It was difficult for anyone to disparage Carman completely; it cannot in all honesty be done. Many younger poets have condemned him because of the legend, and because of the plethora of loyalty to his name and reputation in Fredericton. The younger poets rebelled; and in Canada the younger poets are often the critics. Carman was discarded because his themes and his forms were hackneyed and not applicable to the conditions of the twentieth century.

But despite all the rejection, all the ridicule of the legendary poet who wore turquoise jewelry, Carman's verse did not disappear. He is, along with Robert Service and Pauline Johnson, the most widely anthologized poet in the history of Canadian letters. To group him with Service and Johnson is not to discredit him or to praise him. It shows, however, that his poetry is memorable; it never loses its charm for the reader of anthologies; his most simple lyrics cast a spell on the youngest mind. Carman possessed a gift of the poet but only at times was he able to share his greater artistic insights with his readers. The history of his reputation shows that it cannot be extinguished. His little fire continues to burn. It burns more strongly in Fredericton, but all Canadians acknowledge that the national literature is richer because Carman added to it.

Because the Canadian people needed a poet, they romanticized Bliss Carman, originating a legend that has little basis in fact, or in creative talent. In Canadian literature Carman is, along with Roberts, the leader of the sixties group of poets. He is revered and acclaimed, mostly in New Brunswick where loyalties are strong. Loyalties are not bad, but they must be tempered with reason and truth. Carman was at times a successful poet; he captured moods and atmospheres that are unique. But in the framework both of world and Canadian literature, Carman's is a minor talent.

Carman was a victim of his own colonial background, his own traditional temperament. His personality was shaped more by outside influences than by native inclination. He played the role of a poet well; his greatest contribution to Canadian letters is that he made Canadians aware of poets. Carman was not a careful poet; he was not capable of any degree of self-criticism. Though his poetry may appeal to many people because of its sentiment and its imagery, every poem he wrote has flaws, some more serious than others. Had he devoted more of the time he spent on Unitrinianism and the study of older poets to his own composition, his work would merit a higher position than it does. It is the poetry of a provincial, of a person who seemed to be more concerned with the accouterments of the poet than with poetry itself. His work, as it stands, is often defective in taste and style; some of it is quite commonplace. As verse, his work adds little to Canadian literature except in the occasional lyrics. But his work marked a great beginning, a beginning that led to the flourishing of Canadian poetry in the middle of the twentieth-century. As the literary history of most countries shows, the innovators are often forgotten because of the stature of those who follow.

But is it fair to judge the work of Carman by the standards of world literature? Should his poetry be placed alongside that of his American and British contemporaries and weighed and found wanting? Because he was obviously an imitator, is it fair to judge him by the accomplishments of those he modeled his work after? Or should his verses be considered in reference to their historical context, the beginning of a new movement of poetry in a very young country? An affirmative answer to the second question creates a double standard; right or wrong, it serves as a guide to an understanding and appreciation of the position of Bliss Carman. When compared with his minor American contemporaries, Carman's work is of very equal value. As a conscious imitator he did a good job, even though at times he was unable to see into the core of another poet's work. Often his appreciation of those after whom he modeled his own work was based on false judgments. His understanding of other people's work and of their lives is uncertain.

Carman's reputation is high in Canada because of his position in the sixties group of poets; he initiated a distinctly Canadian poetry through his use of landscape to communicate emotion. But more than that, he is a transitional poet, and as such takes his place in Canadian literature. It is easy to downgrade his work because of the obvious influences of the Romantic and Victorian poets; this has in no way, however, diminished his stature or deprived him of a permanent place in the history of Canadian letters. Though his predecessors are usually called the "transitional" poets, Carman is considered the writer who began the change to a more distinctly Canadian verse. He used the ideas and forms of others, but gave to them a distinctiveness which poets since his time have developed.

Carman's poetry, and all Canadian poetry of the period, is a small branch of English poetry. No matter where one may stand, in London or in Toronto, the poetry of Carman plays a minor position. It has the weaknesses of late nineteenth-century poetry —moralism and heavy sentiment—but few poets of the period ever escaped these. He belongs to his own time; he imitated the best work of the immediate past, and possessed a lyrical quality that was soon exhausted. Though Carman lived until 1929, he does not belong to this century at all; he belongs instead to a provincial phase of the mid-nineteenth century. His social thinking is a parody of Emerson's; his poetry is a concentration of tradition and pseudo-experience. He clings to a romantic respect for the individual while passively acknowledging the social needs of man. The poetry is always naïve, and often personal. It is divided about equally between the more objective pieces, descriptive or narrative, and the subjective, personal lyrics. His work shows something of the traditional United Empire Loyalist addiction to introspection, and he never becomes radically self-conscious or irrational in the use of symbol or image. His poetry has an averageness which often wins for him a sizable audience and accounts for so much of his verse being studied in grade school.

There is nothing startling in the poetry of Bliss Carman; unfortunately he was often unable to bring his thought into focus. He rambles far too much, probably because of his highly romantic sensibility. Fairly conventional ideas are absorbed into his work, and the writers of his own group and those who immediately followed him fell into similar patterns. It was not until the thirties that a new synthesis was found in Canadian poetry, and that depended mainly upon a rejection of what Carman and his group had held high. But Carman had a strong directive influence on the art of poetry in Canada. After Carman other writers in Canada were able to scan a wider horizon if only because the Canadian public was more ready for poets than it had been before.

The success of Bliss Carman's best poems lies partly in their construction, and partly in his lyrical use of language. The poems are always well balanced; parts of stanzas are repeated for emphasis and direction, with other lines often juxtaposed to heighten the emotional effect. Everything he wrote illustrates his lyrical gift. He conveys the feeling of human situations as the lyric poet must, and the poems have a shapeliness and a concentrated diction that makes them well-wrought. Often, too, the poems yield their full meaning only on rereading, when the reader can link the implications of phrases that do not seem related on the first reading. And the good poems illuminate each other; at times an idea may appear to be fragmentary, but it is clarified by other poems. For a while, Carman moves toward a culmination; then, unfortunately, he stops and relies upon repetition to make his theme convincing.

Carman was never assured in his poetry, as he was never assured in his life. He found security in his friendship with Mary Perry King, but it was a false security for it caused stagnation. Her influence over him in a way destroyed him; perhaps he would have been able to develop had he been away from her influence. After his first volume of poetry he rarely wrote with precision; often he seems to have been unsure of the effect he intended. In the end, Carman never learned the secret of the poet—the achievement of the intended effect with precision and an inexplicable rightness.

There is about Carman's work a pervading monotony of tone, a lack of strength, and a slightness of content. His diction and his ideas lack the vigor of a Shelley or a Browning. He was a poet who had very little to say. Yet, there is a characteristic quality to his work, a tone showing a delicacy of expression, a haunting melancholy, and a musical lyricism. Within his own artistic limits he displayed a consistency of expression; he was always able to capture the melody of a mood, the tone of an atmosphere, the color of a setting. And even though his themes are limited, he was able to give a spontaneous quality to his verse. But all this does not make him a great poet; neither does it put him into the category to which he is often assigned, that of a "minor but good" poet. It is the quantity rather than the quality of his verse which gives him a place in a study of Canadian poets. He brought to Canadians an awareness of poetry and of poets.

Carman was a sincere and simple author, who wrote poems showing a unique ability to create a mood. Showing does not necessarily mean displaying. Carman's poems, indeed, make little obvious display at all. That, perhaps, is why many people prefer Canadian poets of the thirties and after. Carman's work is often unlike the production of a man who pretentiously played the role of the poet; it is, rather, simple, sincere, and without affectation. His full appeal is not immediate. The quantity and repetition of his poetry withholds its more subtle pleasures for discriminating admirers. His work needs knowing, knowing with some understanding of the life of the writer; a reader must discard so much of the myth that surrounds the life of Carman. And a reader must go through many poems before one is found that is worthwhile; that makes reading the others more of a challenge than a chore. When Carman does write a good poem, it is admirably done. After the reader has studied Carman's life and work, his poetry becomes very rewarding, not merely because of the number of good poems, but because of the way they combine to produce a rich and varied picture of the range of human experience. When Carman stripped away the affectation—and when his reader discards the myth—his work is a rich expression of common experience. Simplification was his method; simplification is his strength.

Notes and References

Chapter Two

1. Carman, letter to H. D. C. Lee, September 29, 1911, from the Carman Letters, "Edith and Lorne Pierce Collection of Canadiana," Queen's University Library.
2. Carman, "Introduction" to *The Kinship of Nature* (Boston, 1904), p. iii.
3. Lorne Pierce, "Introduction" to *The Selected Poems of Bliss Carman* (Toronto, 1954), pp. 28–29.
4. Carman, letter to Agnes Gale, Queen's University Library.
5. Letter written by Eliza (Mrs. William Whitman) Bailey of New Canaan, Conn., to her niece, Mrs. Margaret Marshall (Bailey) West, located in the Rufus Hatheway Collection, Bonar Law-Bennett Library, University of New Brunswick.
6. Letter to Attorney Dana Hawthorne by Lorne Pierce, November 14, 1940, Bonar Law-Bennett Library, University of New Brunswick.
7. Story told by a librarian at Queen's University Library.
8. Carman, letter to Nancy Carman, April 14, 1892, Bonar Law-Bennett Library, University of New Brunswick.
9. Lorne Pierce, "Introduction," p. 29.
10. Lorne Pierce says that "Some day the full story of this friendship will be told" in his "Introduction" to *The Selected Poems;* he fails to tell it, however, and if he did know it, it appears that he did not leave the story in his private papers.
11. Lorne Pierce, "Introduction," p. 24.

Chapter Three

1. Carman, letter to Nancy Carman, April 14, 1892, Bonar Law-Bennett Library, University of New Brunswick.
2. Carman, *The Friendship of Art* (Boston, 1904), p. 58.
3. *Ibid.*, p. 58.
4. James Cappon, *Bliss Carman* (Toronto, 1930), p. 18
5. *Ibid.*, p. 18.

6. Peter McArthur, "On Having Known a Poet," *The Atlantic Monthly* (May 1906), p. 47.

7. This shows, too, how Carman gets carried away with the intensity of his rhythms; often he creates poems that become monotonous because each stanza is the same, the number of stanzas is too many for the scope of the poem's theme, as in "Spring Song."

8. The lost-lover theme is a prominent one in Carman; here it is not a personal lament but rather one which he feels he should express; it was another poetic convention for him.

9. Here is the lyric intensity of Housman, with a simplicity that becomes deceptive.

10. Duncan Campbell Scott, "The Forsaken," *Canadian Anthology*, ed. Klinck and Watters (Toronto, 1957), p. 147.

11. Their friendship is discussed in the second chapter of this book.

12. James Cappon calls this one of Carman's more successful poems, "remarkable for its wealth of sensuous feeling and fancy" (in his *Bliss Carman*, p. 65). I cannot agree with him.

13. Cappon, p. 63.

14. Carman, letter to H. D. C. Lee, January 4, 1912, Queen's University Library.

15. Carman, letter to H. D. C. Lee, October 12, 1910, Queen's University Library.

16. *Ibid.*

17. Cappon, for instance, and other critics, too.

18. This is discussed in the fourth chapter of this book.

19. This poem was originally printed in *Last Songs from Vagabondia*, and reprinted in *From the Green Book of the Bards.*

20. As Cappon suggests, p. 140.

21. Charles G. D. Roberts, "Introduction" to Bliss Carman's *Sappho: One Hundred Lyrics* (Boston, 1905), p. iii.

22. Cappon, p. 163.

23. All references to the Sappho lyrics are from *Lyra Gnaeca*, translated by J. M. Edmonds (London, 1931), vol. I, pp. 140–307.

24. Carman, *The Friendship of Art*, p. 57.

25. This is discussed toward the end of this third chapter.

26. Carman, *The Kinship of Nature*, p. 129.

27. Carman, *The Friendship of Art*, p. 137.

28. Carman, *The Poetry of Life*, p. 3.

Chapter Four

1. Cappon, p. 41.

2. Odell Shepard, *Bliss Carman* (Toronto, 1923), p. 33: "a syn-

thesis or resolution of these extremes in his last period which saves
what was best in the earlier styles but fuses and tempers it into a new
poetic unity."

3. Carman, letter to his mother, March 29, 1883, Queen's University Library.

4. Carl Y. Conner, *Archibald Lampman—Canadian Poet of Nature* (New York, 1929), p. 128.

5. Carman probably gets some of his addiction to alliteration from Browning, his favorite poet.

6. Desmond Pacey, *Creative Writing in Canada* (Toronto, 1952), p. 44.

7. *Ibid.*, p. 45.

8. Northrop Frye would not agree, as indicated in his *Anatomy of Criticism*.

9. W. H. Auden, in "Introduction" to *A Selection From the Poems of Alfred, Lord Tennyson* (New York, 1944), p. 10.

10. Carman, letter to his mother, January 30, 1883, Queen's University Library.

11. Charles G. D. Roberts, "Bliss Carman," *Dalhousie Review* (1929–30), 9:4:3.

Selected Bibliography

PART 1: WORKS OF BLISS CARMAN IN CHRONOLOGICAL ORDER

Low Tide on Grand Pré: A Book of Lyrics. New York: Charles L. Webster, 1893.

Songs From Vagabondia (with Richard Hovey). Boston: Copeland and Day, 1894.

Behind the Arras: A Book of the Unseen. Boston: Lamson, Wolffe, and Company, 1895.

A Seamark: A Threnody For Robert Louis Stevenson. Boston: Lamson, Wolffe, and Company, 1895.

More Songs From Vagabondia (with Richard Hovey). Boston: Lamson, Wolffe, and Company, 1896.

Ballads of Lost Haven. Boston: Lamson, Wolffe, and Company, 1897.

By the Aurelian Wall, and Other Elegies. Boston: Lamson, Wolffe, and Company, 1898.

A Winter Holiday. Boston: Lamson, Wolffe, and Company, 1899.

Last Songs From Vagabondia (with Richard Hovey). Boston: Small, Maynard, and Company, 1900.

Ballads and Lyrics: A Selection. London: A. H. Bullen Press, 1902.

Ode on the Coronation of King Edward. Boston: L. C. Page and Company, 1902.

From the Book of Myths (Pipes of Pan Series, No. I). Boston: L. C. Page and Company, 1902.

From the Green Book of the Bards (Pipes of Pan Series, No. II). Boston: L. C. Page and Company, 1903.

Songs of the Sea Children (Pipes of Pan Series, No. III). Boston: ton: L. C. Page and Company, 1904.

Songs From a Northern Garden (Pipes of Pan Series, No. IV). Boston: ton: L. C. Page and Company, 1904.

The Kinship of Nature. Boston: L. C. Page and Company, 1904.

The Friendship of Art. Boston: L. C. Page and Company, 1904.

From the Book of Valentines (Pipes of Pan Series, No. V). Boston: L. C. Page and Company, 1905.

Sappho: One Hundred Lyrics. Boston: L. C. Page and Company, 1905.

The Poetry of Life. Boston: L. C. Page and Company, 1905.

The Pipes of Pan (Definitive Edition). Boston: L. C. Page and Company, 1906.

The Making of the Personality (Essays, with Mary Perry King). Boston: L. C. Page and Company, 1908.

The Rough Rider and Other Poems. New York: Mitchell and Kennerley, 1909.

Echoes From Vagabondia. Boston: Small, Maynard and Company, 1912.

Daughters of Dawn: A Lyrical Pageant (with Mary Perry King). New York: Mitchell and Kennerley, 1913.

Earth's Deities: and Other Rhythmic Masques (with Mary Perry King). New York: Mitchell and Kennerley, 1914.

April Airs—A Book of New England Lyrics. Boston: Small, Maynard and Company, 1916.

Later Poems. Toronto: McClelland and Stewart, 1921.

Far Horizons. Boston: Small, Maynard, and Company, 1925.

Talks on Poetry and Life. Toronto: The Ryerson Press, 1926.

Wild Garden. Boston: Dodd, Mead, and Company, 1929.

Sanctuary. Boston: Dodd, Mead, and Company, 1929.

Bliss Carman's Poems. Boston: Dodd, Mead, and Company, 1931.

The Music of Earth. Toronto: The Ryerson Press, 1931.

Bliss Carman's Scrap Book. Toronto: The Ryerson Press, 1931.

The Selected Poems of Bliss Carman, Edited and with an Introduction by Lorne Pierce. Toronto: McClelland and Stewart, 1954.

PART 2: LETTERS AND MANUSCRIPTS OF BLISS CARMAN

"Letters of Bliss Carman," located in the Hatheway Collection, Bonar Law-Bennett Library, University of New Brunswick.

"Manuscripts of Bliss Carman," located in the Hatheway Collection, Bonar Law-Bennett Library, University of New Brunswick.

"Photostat Manuscripts of Bliss Carman," located in the Hatheway Collection, Bonar Law-Bennett Library, University of New Brunswick.

"Scrapbooks with Newspaper Articles About Bliss Carman," located in the Hatheway Collection, Bonar Law-Bennett Library, University of New Brunswick.

"Press Reviews of Bliss Carman," located in the Hatheway Collection, Bonar Law-Bennett Library, University of New Brunswick.

"Bliss Carman Letters to His Mother, January 30, 1883 to August 27,

1885," *Edith and Lorne Pierce Collection of Canadiana* (on microfilm), located in Queen's University Library.

PART 3: BOOKS ABOUT BLISS CARMAN

CAPPON, JAMES. *Bliss Carman.* Toronto: Ryerson, 1930.

LEE, H. D. C. *Bliss Carman: A Study in Canadian Literature.* Thesis for Doctorate, Université de Rennes. Boston: Herald Printing Company, 1912.

MILLER, MURIEL. *Bliss Carman: A Portrait.* Toronto: Ryerson, 1935.

SHEPARD, ODELL. *Bliss Carman.* Toronto: McClelland and Stewart, 1923.

PART 4: BOOKS CONTAINING ARTICLES OR REFERENCES TO
BLISS CARMAN

ARCHER, WILLIAM. "Bliss Carman," *Poets of the Younger Generation,* London: Barker, 1902.

BROWN, E. K. *On Canadian Poetry.* Toronto: Ryerson, 1943.

COLUM, PADRAIC. Prefatory note in *Sanctuary* by Bliss Carman. Boston: Dodd, Mead, and Company, 1929.

GARVIN, J. W. *Canadian Poets.* Toronto: McClelland and Stewart, 1926.

HATHEWAY, R. H. "An Appreciation," in *Later Poems* by Bliss Carman. Toronto: McClelland and Stewart, 1921.

HIND, C. LEWIS. "Bliss Carman," in *More Authors and I.* London: Barker, 1922.

MACMURCHY, ARCHIBALD. *Handbook of Canadian Literature.* Toronto: Ryerson, 1906.

MAXWELL, L. M. B. *The River St. John and its Poets.* Sackville: Tribune Press, 1947.

PACEY, DESMOND. *Creative Writing In Canada.* Toronto: Ryerson, 1952.

PERCIVAL, W. P., ed. *Leading Canadian Poets.* Toronto: Ryerson, 1948.

PIERCE, LORNE. *An Outline of Canadian Literature.* Toronto: Ryerson, 1927.

———. *Three Fredericton Poets.* Toronto: Ryerson, 1933.

RHODENIZER, V. B. *Handbook of Canadian Literature.* Ottawa: Graphic Publishers, 1930.

RITTENHOUSE, JESSIE B. "Bliss Carman," *Younger American Poets.* Boston: L. C. Page and Company, 1905.

ROBERTS, CHARLES G. D. Introduction to *Sappho: One Hundred Lyrics* by Bliss Carman. Boston: L. C. Page and Company, 1905.

PART 5: ARTICLES IN PERIODICALS ABOUT BLISS CARMAN

EDGAR, PELHAM. "In Canadian Poetry," *Acta Victoriana* (February 1922), 198–200.

GRAY, G. "Mystery of Bliss Carman's Ashes," *MacLean's Magazine* (August 1, 1951), 40.

HATHEWAY, R. H. "Bliss Carman—Poet of the Sea," *The Sailor* (July 1920), 19–20.

———. "Carman's Books," *Acadie* (April 15, 1930), 4–6.

LAWRENCE, M. I. "In Memory of Bliss Carman," *Canadian Home Journal* (June 1930), 29–31.

LEISNER, A. R. "Bliss Carman's 'The Girl in the Poster,' " *Acadie* (June 1, 1930), 11.

———. "Carman's 'Spring Song,' " *Acadie* (April 15, 1930), 6–7.

———. "Carman's 'The Mendicants,' " *Acadie* (May 15, 1930), 5–6.

MACKAY, L. A. "Bliss Carman," *Canadian Forum* (February 1933), 182–3.

MCARTHUR, PETER. "On Having Known a Poet," *The Atlantic Monthly* (May 1906), 45–9.

PACEY, DESMOND. "Bliss Carman: A Reappraisal," *Northern Review* (February-March 1950), 2–10.

———. "Bliss Carman." *Ten Canadian Poets.* Toronto: Ryerson, 1958. 59–113.

ROBERTS, CHARLES G. D. "Some Reminiscences of Carman in New York," *Canadian Poetry Magazine* (December 1940), 5–10.

———. "Bliss Carman," *Dalhousie Review* (January 1929), 9:409–417.

———. "More Reminiscences of Bliss Carman," *Dalhousie Review* (February 1930), 10:1–9.

———. "Carman and His Own Country," *Acadie* (April 15, 1930), 2–4.

ROSS, MALCOLM. "A Symbolic Approach to Carman," *The Canadian Bookman* (December 1932), 140–144.

STRINGER, ARTHUR. "Canadians in New York—America's Foremost Lyricist," *National Monthly of Canada* (January 1904), 3–5.

VAN PATTEN, G. "Bliss Carman and the Bibliophile," *Queen's Quarterly* (December 1925), 202–205.

WADE, H. G. "The Bard of Mount and Moor," *The Canadian Bookman* (February 1927), 39–40.

Index